Man Confronts Himself Alone

Man Confronts Himself Alone

Hannah Arendt and the Entanglements
of Science, Technology, Economics,
and Politics in Modern Life

ZOHAR MIHAELY

WIPF & STOCK · Eugene, Oregon

MAN CONFRONTS HIMSELF ALONE
Hannah Arendt and the Entanglements of Science, Technology,
Economics, and Politics in Modern Life

Wipf & Stock
An Imprint of Wipf and Stock Publishers
199 W. 8th Ave., Suite 3
Eugene, OR 97401

www.wipfandstock.com

PAPERBACK ISBN: 979-8-3852-2732-7
HARDCOVER ISBN: 979-8-3852-2733-4
EBOOK ISBN: 979-8-3852-2734-1

VERSION NUMBER 10/09/24

For my parents Micky and Victor.

I am deeply grateful to
Dr. Gil Mihaely and Prof. Jerome Kohn
for reviewing a draft of the manuscript
and providing valuable feedback.

Contents

Introduction

IT IS CUSTOMARY TO call the period in which we live today in late modernity "the age of technology," "technoscience," etc., because of the unprecedented rate of development of technology and science and their dominant presence in all areas of our lives, which is only increasing.[1] In recent decades, this has led to a literary—scientific and popular—flood on this topic, which in general can be divided into two approaches: utopian, which sees it as, if not the fulfillment of redemption, at least the path to it, with a futuristic tone; for example, among post-humanists, high-tech people, and scientists of exact sciences. And dystopian, which sees it as a serious deterioration in relation to the present, an approach with an apocalyptic tone.[2]

In the present book, I discuss Hannah Arendt's considerations on this topic in the fifties and early sixties,[3] which offer

1. Today there is such a feeling that technology is the door to the future, meaning that it will save us. Many feel uncomfortable with the fact that they know nothing about it but also feel they have to get into it somehow, take courses, etc. This phenomenon is unprecedented in history.

2. In pure academic discourse, it is common to use the expression "technoscience" for technology and science because of the difficulty of separating them in everyday reality. But there are also thinkers who focus on one of them and those who jump between both.

3. Her main work that deals with science and technology—that is, with the question of what has happened to the human condition since the modern age—is the book *The Human Condition* (1958), in the prologue and the last part called "The Active Life and the Modern Era." Her other works that correspond with key points from *The Human Condition* are the collection

enlightening critical tools for thinking about science and politics from an approach that combines feelings of despair and hope.[4]

Arendt's *The Human Condition*, the main source for my investigation here, is essentially about alienation from the world as expressed through the relationship between science, technology, and politics. At the basis of the thesis in this book is the premise that throughout recorded history, for more than two thousand years, the human condition has been characterized by a split. On the one hand, humans are earthly creatures; we were born into a world that is beyond our control, and like the rest of the living creatures, we are subject to fate. On the other hand, we built an artificial world within nature according to our will and image. This is the political world. The split manifests itself in the fact that we are not completely free, yet we mortals have built our own world that will endure after our death. However, man also had a wish from time immemorial to escape this human condition and disconnect himself from his bond to Earth. The conditions for the

---

Between Past and Future (1961), in the articles "The Concept of History"— which expands and deepens the concept of "the process"—and "The Conquest of Space and the Stature of Man," which is another attempt to think about what has happened to man in the age of modern science and technology. All these discussions connect to her reflections on totalitarianism in her first major book, *The Origins of Totalitarianism* (1951); for example, the use of science and technology by totalitarian regimes from the conception that "everything is possible" and the theme of the appearance of "human rights" in the Second World War, which links to the rise of the animal laborers and the rise of the ideal of life as a supreme value.

4. Arendt's interest in science began with her investigations of totalitarianism. The central feature of the totalitarian imagination was a biological understanding of humanity. Leading politics according to a model of natural processes was a common denominator for Nazism and Stalinism, namely seeing the regime as a harmonious cause of natural law that enables the laws of race or class to make humanity an active bearer of natural law. That, of course, was a threat to political culture. However, it seems like the discourse on Arendt's thought always revolves around the topic of totalitarianism in a way that marginalizes her treatment of science and technology. Thus, it should be noted that during the fifties she reacted to a political-cultural situation dominated by scientific and technological changes, which, rather than the barbarism of totalitarianism, were the reasons for the overthrow of the distinction between nature and the human history.

realization of this dream have matured through modern science with the invention of instruments (telescopes) by means of which man moved the center point from the earth to space. For some time now, modern scientists have been talking about the emergence of a new human species a century from now that will be completely free, which means that the human condition as we know it is about to change into something else. Indeed, much of it is already a reality. The new universal science born from Galileo's discoveries enabled man to insert cosmic forces into the household of nature—for example, the splitting of the atom and the fabrication of new man-made materials.

Yet, in Arendt's account, the entire modern scientific project is hypothetical in its entirety. Galileo's victory in realizing that the earth is not an absolute center was accompanied by a sense of embarrassment and a growing lack of faith in the reality perceived by the senses and in the notions of truth and certainty. In response, rationality and reason have become modern thought's unwavering pillars. As Descartes put it, "I think, therefore I exist" with absolute certainty. This method, coupled with the idea that the only way to know the truth about nature is through mathematics, gave rise to a new experimental science in which scientists formulate their hypotheses, organize their experiments, and use those experiments to verify those very hypotheses. Meaning that science cannot say anything about the behavior of nature per se, but only reports the impressions of the instruments on it. Hence, technology is employed to "prove" that the craziest abstract scientific concepts that mathematics allows by its nature can be applied with "results." Thus, the hypotheses are "authentic." It simply works! Arendt concludes that this is a sign that thought has separated from reality. Scientists are capable of doing things that they do not understand.

The question, according to Arendt, is, What does this mean for our humanity?[5] Does it increase human stature? Arendt reminds us that it is not a scientific question because the technology to execute it is there, but a political one, meaning something that each of us should decide if we really want to conform with

5. Arendt, *Between Past and Future*, 260.

science's adoption of the place of God in an attempt to expand our traditional man-made political world to literally all the earth, that is, to recreate nature—with the risk of destroying it completely—and move even further in space as far as we can reach. Arendt saw a striking description of where we have arrived at in the words of physicist Werner Heisenberg: "Man confronts himself alone." And remarked on this: "The astronaut, shot into outer space and imprisoned in his instrument-ridden capsule where each actual physical encounter with his surroundings would spell immediate death, might well be taken as the symbolic incarnation of Heisenberg's man—the man who will be the less likely ever to meet anything but himself and man-made things."[6]

At the same time, what is actually wrong with changing the human condition? What is wrong with the comfort that modern science has undoubtedly brought with it? Well, Arendt is not opposed to the progress of science and technology per se. She appreciates their astonishing, unprecedented achievements in modernity. But in her opinion, there is something more important than pride in human triumph over the boundaries of nature, or comfort. Specifically, our political culture. And this is where science and technology pose a threat.

Modern science's adoption of a worldview from an Archimedean point in the universe, which allows us to regard Earth as merely another optional detail in a big picture as if we were the inhabitants of some planet in the universe, is a package deal. On the one hand, an Archimedean point, as its name indicates, allowed man to gain unprecedented control over earthly nature in the first place. However, such control is only possible if man distances himself from the world, which is another way of saying he alienates himself from it. This universal science transformed the human world into a laboratory in which the potentiality of cosmic processes to destroy not only every human artifice but also humanity as such is tested. Indeed, scientists became actors with enormous political power.

6. Arendt, *Between Past and Future*, 271–72.

This brought about a series of dramatic reversals of social, economic, and political priorities in modernity that eventually degraded human society to the lowest level ever. A mass society that cultivates behaviorism, indifference to the immediate environment, thoughtlessness, and cares only about private interests—in short, it lacks all the human capacities necessary for the building of the political culture that Arendt values and advocates through all her writings, namely participatory democracy. And if this is not enough, we are preached to love this kind of people and idealize their needs.

In view of the continuing intervention in nature and society according to scientific laws in liberal democratic countries today, that promotes the technocracy of the social sphere, the awareness and responsibility that Arendt expects from the ordinary citizen is not a simple matter. This universally alienated attitude dominates both governments and mass society, the consumer society that in fact enjoys the toys and comfort that technology provides.

Despite everything, Arendt believes that humanity has not completely lost its ability to change the world. Although the highest activity—political action—has become perverted, the ability to act exists. Yet those who are still able to act in the authentic sense of starting something new, albeit poorly, are not the professional politicians but rather the scientists, that small minority who have always operated far from the spotlight and whose opinion was not considered by the majority. But according to Arendt, the fate of politics must not be left in their hands because they act from a point of view that is outside the world, and therefore it is not possible to derive a common historical meaning from their action. Since the "modern world" is already profoundly shaped by technoscience, meaning that we moderns have developed an irreversible dependence on technology, the task of political theory today, according to Arendt, is to challenge the epistemic authority of science and the attempt to implement it in politics and society, through the creation of ways to redefine human activity so that it becomes worldly again within these circumstances.

Finally, some readers might question Arendt's considerations on science and technology from sixty years ago. Apparently, it seems that the examples she provides, such as the Sputnik satellite or Galileo's telescope,[7] remind us of the simplicity of the examples that her teacher Martin Heidegger[8] brought in his discussion on technology: a hammer, a silver chalice, a wind farm, etc., which seem to be more suitable for the industrial age at the beginning of modernity than for the post-industrial society with its information technology, communication (e.g., television), hi-tech, and more. In my opinion, one of Arendt's contributions to the ongoing discourse on science and technology is offering an unusual perspective that, against the prevalent premise that the fundamental struggle underlying Western modernity is that between religion and science, suggests that the real conflict is between politics and science. Hence, Arendt indicates that although we live today in a world where it is not possible to talk about politics without referring to science and technology, science and politics are unable to communicate with each other, not because of bad public education but due to the nature of modern science. Secondly, Arendt's reading of modern physics in the fifties places her within contemporary debates about humanism and post-humanism, which have been ongoing since the end of the Second World War. However, it is important to recall that Arendt's concern is alienation from the political world, and not from the world in a natural sense. Thus, those interested in current concerns of climate change, ecology, environment, and similar topics may find themselves disappointed by Arendt's usage of the term "nature" in her study of science. Arendt did not consider nature in terms of, say, endangered animal protection and the climate crisis, nor did she regard it as a solution to the problem of alienation from the world, in contrast to the romantic perspective taken by Rousseau up to the hippie movement.

7. Galileo's telescope belongs to the so-called first revolution of lenses, while we live today after the second revolution that crossed the limits of optics, such as X-rays, radio images, etc.

8. Heidegger did not view technology as inherently bad. In fact, he believed it to be capable of "disclosure." However, he had no interest in politics and was just concerned with Being. This distinguishes him from Arendt.

According to her political theory, the twentieth-century growth of authoritarian deterministic ideology was made possible by contemporary appeals to nature. This regime's faith in "revealing the meaning of nature" and bending it to fit its policies is precisely what makes it so fundamentally wicked.

The fact that Arendt considers the problems she raises to be of political interest at the civil level shows her known desire for a dialogue with a wide audience. At the same time, her insights were communicated in a book, *The Human Condition*, that is considered her most complicated, even for experienced scholars. The present book is basically a rereading of the last chapter of Arendt's book, combining insights from her relevant essays that correspond with it. It opens with a review of the main elements in Arendtian thought, starting with what can be called her "neo-Aristotelian post-Marxist" phenomenological conceptualization of the active life of man (from the middle sections of *The Human Condition*), which is her unique and constant reference for understanding human existence as a political process in any subject she approaches and therefore an essential theoretical background for her views on science and technology. In general, my purpose is to reproduce the stages of Arendt's line of thought and to articulate the conclusions that the logic of these stages led her to, most of which have already been described here.

Theoretical Background

The Human Condition

ARENDT'S POLITICAL THEORY FOCUSES on the historical and contemporary condition of humanity's existence in the world as a political process. In contrast to the "human nature" that philosophers throughout history believed in, Arendt was of the opinion that there is no such thing.[1] According to her, "human condition" means the conditions that determine the range of possibilities for the existence of humanity. This perception becomes clear in her conceptualization of the "active life" that she picked from Marx.[2]

THE ACTIVE LIFE

Arendt examined the conditions of human existence through an investigation of the "active life" (Latin: *vita activa*). It consists of three fundamental human activities: *labor*, related to the satisfaction of man's biological and material needs; *work*, which concerns the production of sustainable tools and objects; and *action*, which

1. Arendt, *Human Condition*, 12.

2. In the mid-fifties, Arendt worked in European libraries on a study she called "Totalitarian Foundations of Marxism," intended to complete her great work, *The Origins of Totalitarianism*. Between 1958–1962 she published three books: *The Human Condition*, *Between Past and Future*, and *On Revolution*, all of which grew out of the line of thought of what was supposed to be the book on Marxism, which was never written.

is the collection of human engagements that create a society—that is, politics. These activities have three parallel mentalities—namely, *animal laborans* ("the working animal" or "the toiler"), *homo faber* ("tool-man" or man as producer and creator), and the *man of action* (or the political actor), respectively. *Labor* has an infinite circular nature; all its products are intended for one-time consumption—for example, bread, whose function is only survival, which leads to further and repeated labor as in nature. Therefore, it expresses the animal aspect of man. Redemption from the cycle of survival comes from the *work* of *homo faber*, since the tools he produces do not just lighten the burden of work, they leave a permanent mark on the world. The greatness of the tractor is not that it helps the plowing so much as it can be used over and over again.[3]

But even the products of *homo faber* have a flaw: they have no meaning in themselves. Without the farmer, the tractor is nothing more than a random collection of metal parts. And so, just as the *work* redeems the *labor*, the *action* redeems the *work*, because the existence of a person as part of society is what gives meaning to both his creation and his survival. *Action* is the only element of "active life" that depends on human pluralism—being social creatures who live and communicate with each other in groups. Both the *labor* and the *work* can be done by only one person, but not so for the building of relationships and the establishment of a society that requires the presence of others. Arendt emphasized that this pluralism was already mentioned in the story of the creation of man in the Bible: "Male and female created He them,"[4] and that in the society of ancient Rome, which in her opinion was the most political nation in history, the terms "to live" and "to be in

3. As soon as man began to establish structures between himself and nature, he became *homo faber*, the productive man. While labor adapts itself to the endless circular rhythm of life from birth to death, work activity offers limited control over nature and a measure of stability against the incessant flow of nature. The work is artificial. Through it, man surrounds himself with manufactured products and thus builds a world that, even if it is not immortal, at least lasts longer than human life. Without this stable world, there would be no space or stage for the human drama to take place.

4. Gen 1:27.

the company of humans" were synonymous words. Public *action*, speech, and politics were, for Arendt, the pinnacle of "active life."

The political action that includes speech and deeds is therefore the right form of activity that transcends necessity and instrumentality, an activity that is not intended to maintain biological life but to serve as a platform for developing meaning for public life. In speech, there is no coercion or violence but a peaceful life through persuasion with words between opinions. This was the political culture in the ancient Greek polis (city-state). For the citizens of the polis, command and coercion instead of persuasion with words is a pre-political form that dominated outside the polis in the barbarian culture and in the household within the polis. Real speech and discourse are not limited to a specific topic in particular—health matters, for example. Speech is not aimed at a goal, because political action has no purpose other than its very performance. Only speech frees people beyond biological existential necessity toward moral and political judgment. Therefore, where there is talk of common matters, there is correct politics (or "the political"). The Greeks, like other civilized peoples, judged human behavior according to moral standards that took into account intentions and emotions. But for them, the ultimate evaluation of the action is done only according to the measure of greatness because, by its nature, it strives for the unusual, the original that breaks the conventions accepted by many in everyday routine life. From here, Arendt distinguishes between an activity that is carried out in order to achieve another goal (utility, "in order to") versus an activity for its own sake, the *action*. Arendt criticized the philosophers throughout the Western tradition, starting with the Greeks, who mostly chose to focus on the "spiritual life" or "contemplative life" (Latin: *vita contemplativa*) and considered them superior to the "active life." While the philosophers were working, the preoccupation with "active life" only hindered them from fulfilling their duties. Her critique was also directed at medieval Christian Scholasticism, which turned its back on the world and politics in favor of a "life of contemplation" and an expectation of the world "behind the curtain," thus abandoning the public sphere where political activity takes place.

To sum up, Arendt's entire political theory strives for a formula of limited government, i.e., participatory democracy. Contrary to the prejudice that politics is ultimately only government, according to Arendt, mere government is not political because it imposes a monopoly on speech and action, something that destroys pluralism. When the *action* is reserved for a dictator or a ruling clique, then there are no citizens but only masters and subjects whose only goal is the preservation of life and the power to rule. The actions of the citizens have meaning only within this goal.

THE PRIVATE AND THE PUBLIC SPHERES

The second element in Arendt's discussion of the "human condition" is her distinction between the (ancient Greek) polis model and the household, public and private—that is, between what is given to us naturally and the public artifice in which we create things together. The household—the private world that focuses on the preservation of life—is the place where we set boundaries between us and the world. However, although the public world is what we share together, we also need a private space because it is impossible to live in constant transparency and to be exposed to the bright light of the presence of others for a long time. We need a place to hide, for example, feelings of love or kindness, because if they are too public, they will lose their value. To enter the public world and discover "who we are," a certain space is needed in which the person will secretly develop as an individual, a home which will help him surprise others when he enters the public space. Hence, the household establishes the public sphere in a certain way.

In contrast to the household as a place where we preserve life—the realm of necessity, a place where activities take place in silence, such as birth, death, mating, etc.—the polis represents what we hold in common, the realm of freedom and equality. The polis—the political domain—is for Arendt an artificial space, hence equality (in politics) is not natural. Against Hobbes and all the liberal philosophers who held that humans are equal by nature, Arendt claims that the artificial achievement of politics is to make us equal, contrary to the necessity and inequality that exist in private life and the household. Equality in the public sphere means living among our fellows, and therefore it is not related to social justice in an economic sense in the style of Marx, for example. Equality is like freedom—namely, to be free from inequality and rule. We enter the public sphere, the artificial political world that we have built for ourselves within nature on earth, as citizens, where we can discuss and argue as equal citizens that no one has more power than others. The only difference between us is our personal ability—the skill of each one to speak and act in a way that will convince others.

According to Arendt, historically there has always been a distinction between the public-political and the private spheres— that is, between the world of the polis and the world of preserving and maintaining life (the household). Crossing this gap required courage.[5] It was part of being human to occasionally cross the line from the private to the public and become a citizen in public. In the ancient polis, the space of political action was the marketplace (Greek: *agora*) where everyone could break out of their private sphere to be heard and seen by others. As soon as others like a certain action and agree on its greatness or beauty, they will remember and talk about it, and thus, it becomes something that makes their world common. We quote famous poems, talk about cultural heroes and statesmen, and mention architectural works and works of art known to everyone. Discourse and dispute about the direction of collective action require minimal agreement from a maximum of perspectives of the citizens. In other words, a certain communality is needed for the existence of a political body.[6]

5. According to Arendt, the highest political value is courage because it motivates us to leave the private realm of our necessity for the world of politics, where we are exposed to the possibility of not succeeding or not being convinced, and even to death, as in the case of Socrates.

6. This is not about an overly intimate relationship, like love in the early Christian community. Too much love, like too much alienation, threatens

The content of the speech is the political game itself. Politics must first be concerned with itself, the preservation of a free space for action and speech, a place to be heard and seen—that is, the existence of the *agora*. The rest of the content changes depending on the circumstances—not necessarily socioeconomic issues, but always about how different and special people can live together. The content is secondary to the spirit and structure of the political action. The quality of the speech or deed depends on the players' desire to enter the game and leave personal interests in the private sphere, including the interests of groups and even moral claims. A quality political game occurs when the players give themselves completely to it without letting personal motives dictate the game. According to Arendt, sadly, not only in a totalitarian regime and a household ruled by the tyranny of the landlord, but also in a representative regime, the spaces of freedom for civil political activity are limited.

THE RISE OF "THE SOCIAL"

One of the defining characteristics of modernity, according to Arendt, is what she calls "the social," which occurred when the public-political world was subsumed under the private sphere during the eighteenth and nineteenth centuries; that is, there is a blurring of the border between the private and public domains.[7] The roots of "the social" go back and are intertwined with the rise of capitalism. The first attack on the public sphere came in the form of a "property owners' organization" that, instead of striving for access to the public sphere because of their wealth, demanded protection of their private sphere in order to accumulate more wealth. This was important because, in addition to the new "concept of history" in a production format, the traditional status of wealth was replaced by a semi-biological process of endless growth and

politics. A shared world is supposed to be objective. The correct relationship is therefore "friendship," as Aristotle argued.

7. The idea of "the rise of the social" is discussed at length in Arendt's book *On Revolution*.

expansion.[8] As we shall see later, what remains of the permanent is not stable structures erected by the traditional *work* of the *homo faber*, but the omnipresence of biology. The basic existence of capitalism is designed to satisfy and nurture physical needs by things with a transitory character.

The ancient Greeks, who separated the public world of the polis from the private space of the household, did not know of a space designed to satisfy private bodily needs and live collectively. For them, "private" had a negative connotation: living in darkness subject to the pain and boredom of consumption for the sake of survival for the sake of consumption again. While for them "equality" was understood as an equal right to participate in the public sphere, in modernity, equality is the essence of the new "social" domain—that is, it is derived from physical existence and is a goal and not a means to achieve uniqueness and excellence. The social domain, in which "the social" established its public area, released an unnatural growth of the natural, so to speak. And against this growth, the private and public spheres are unable to defend themselves. Like the private sphere, "the social" sphere tends toward regulative behaviorism over action—which is by definition unpredictable and disrupts the normal by the unusual—and therefore *action* is seen as a destabilizing factor. Society members expect certain behaviors from individuals and impose rules to control their behavior.[9] And above all, society depends on standardization and a lack of change in function. In short, society respects the instrumental nature of the function without change. I will elaborate on the phenomenon of "the social" in the last part of the present book, which deals with the rise of mass society, which is another name for "the social."

So far for the main categories that make up Arendt's phenomenological analysis of the "human condition," or human history as a political process. To this I will add another important element, historiosophical, which also appears in the book *The Human*

---

8. Property has been replaced by the accumulation of wealth. It is connected to the concept of "the process," which will be discussed later.

9. This topic is the backbone of Michel Foucault's genealogical investigations.

Condition; Arendt elaborates on it more in the essay "The Concept of History," which is necessary for our discussion here—namely, her distinction between immortality and eternity.

IMMORTALITY

The idea of an eternal, timeless, and "unworldly" truth is fundamentally different from the idea of "immortality," through which the Greeks, Egyptians, and other ancient cultures understood humanity and human truth in the period before the post-Socratic philosophers, according to which the gods live forever and humans are finite beings that can nevertheless build things like states, works of art, and people that will last forever. A person has the ability to upgrade himself to immortality, to a kind of God level, through creating art, politics, nations, or any other physical and spiritual objects that endure, and their memory will be preserved in history. This does not say that some people are not human. Everyone has this potential, but not everyone acts in a manner that realizes it in a way that deserves to be preserved and remembered collectively. According to Arendt, only the best, the *aristoi*, are truly human in the sense that they work for the public and not to get rich or enhance their private happiness. They strive for immortality by doing great things and participating in a public world that will be remembered. In other words, they act in a way that matters to others who will respond to their action and say, "Oh, I like it!" or "I will tell a story about it," or "I see what I have in common with what you do or say."[10] Unlike *labor*, in *action* there is a sense of happiness in starting something new and breaking conventions. It is human to do something surprising. As mentioned, among the Greeks the evaluation of the *action* is done only according to the measure of its greatness, the originality.

10. Obviously, not every speech (opinion) or act is suitable for the public sphere. There are enough quarrelsome and uneducated people out there. Only people with talent can participate in politics, which makes it sometimes a bit elitist. Indeed, Arendt's competitive Olympic style was criticized as being akin to Nietzsche's.

CHAPTER 1

The Emergence of Modernity

ALIENATION FROM THE WORLD

MODERNITY, AS ARENDT NARRATES it, is a complex and dynamic period that is divided into two parts, the second of which is the "modern age" from the middle of the sixteenth century to the middle of the twentieth century, when the "modern world" we live in today began. This periodicity is characterized by two developments: "world alienation," namely, the alienation of the moderns from the "space in between" that separates and relates people to each other and to nature, which concerns places, institutions, laws, practices, and customs where politics takes place. And alienation from the earth, meaning their alienation from the existential situation that makes them earthly beings. Arendt calls these phenomena together: "twofold flight from the earth."[1]

The transition to the "modern age," the first phase of modernity, was not brought about by ideas but by three unexpected events[2] with consequences that surprised even their forerunners—

1. Arendt, *Human Condition*, 6.

2. Arendt applied her category of "event" to the history of science. For her, events were constellations of human actions and unexpected consequences, unexplained by causality alone but capable of starting chains of further events that enabled the identification of "an unbroken continuity, in which precedents exist and predecessors can be named." The telescope and Galileo's subsequent discoveries, along with the discovery of America and the exploration of the

namely, the study of the planet and the discovery of America; the Reformation and the dispossession of peasant lands; and the invention of the telescope. These events, which are parallel to what is commonly called "the revolution of modern science," gave rise to a branching of events entangled in science, technology, and capital, which intensified man's alienation from the world.[3] However, they are not equal in their importance. The result of the Reformation and the discovery of America was immediate and visible to all. The third event, Galileo's discoveries through the newly invented telescope machine, was only understood by a small group of scientists at the time and was abstract compared to the other two. Yet its influence, which reached its full potential only in the twentieth century in the "modern world," was ultimately the most influential on "the human condition" in that it led to further alienation—to the earth itself—and a dramatic change in man's relationship with nature. Arendt presents these three events as the foundation of modern world alienation; that is, they distance us from the common world, and mark the loss of truth and a shared center. In fact, all other discussions here stem from these events.[4]

---

earth, were "events," though not in the same way as political phenomena such as the French Revolution.

3. The technology of exploring the planet (and the development of transportation) reduced the distances in the world, making us inhabitants of the planet rather than of our particular place within it. The expropriation process started by the Reformation deprived people of their land and their place in the world. Galileo's discovery of the continuity between the movement of the earth and the universe distances people from their world by showing that the view of the world as the center of the earth is disconnected from reality and that the sun does not rise and set as it seems. Science is taking us even further away from the world by unleashing processes on earth that used to occur only very far away from us in the universe (such as nuclear fusion).

4. Some would argue that this alleged selectivity in Arendt's historical arguments, which leaves large parts of humanity, i.e., anyone who is not a westerner, out of the game, stems from her Eurocentrism. But I think this claim can be doubted. According to Francis Fukuyama, the scientific method of modern natural science became accessible to all rational mankind, regardless of culture or nationality. This universal historical change is influenced by military competition. Modern natural science is a decisive military advantage for societies that can develop and produce technology efficiently. The possibility of war

THE DISCOVERY OF THE NEW WORLD AND THE EXPLORATION OF THE EARTH

To describe the first event of the discovery of land and the subsequent exploration of the entire planet, Arendt uses the example of the American continent.[5] The premise of the Age of Discovery was that we would discover new worlds and make the world bigger. But when you map it and calculate distances, the world becomes comprehensible and measurable and therefore loses its size and shrinks. Arendt's description of the "discovery of America" as a colonial effort indicates a long-term process of objectification of the planet that ended only in the twentieth century, at the end of the "modern age," when "man [took] full possession of his mortal dwelling place and gathered the infinite horizons, which were temptingly and forbiddingly open to all previous ages, into a globe whose outlines and detailed surface he knows as he knows the lines in the palm of his hand."[6] However, as mentioned, in the process of exploring the boundaries of the planet Earth, it reached its simultaneous contraction into a "globe" that can be held in the hand and placed as a decoration on the desk. For Arendt, the earth is the most basic condition for the existence of humanity. With the advent of modernity, this condition was marginalized as the idea of earthiness was replaced by a process of objectification through which the land became an object to be transcended. The objectification of the earth indicates that the decisive contraction of the earth "is like a symbol for the general phenomenon that any decrease of terrestrial distance can be won only at the price of putting a decisive distance between man and the earth, of alienating man from his immediate earthly surroundings."[7]

---

forces societies to rationalize and restore their social systems, such as upgrading education systems to create an elite capable of implementing technology infrastructure. The continuation of war and military competition paradoxically unifies nations by forcing them to accept modern technological civilization and social structures. Fukuyama, *End of History*, 72–76.

5. I follow sections 35 and 36 in the last part of *The Human Condition*.

6. Arendt, *Human Condition*, 227.

7. Arendt, *Human Condition*, 228.

THE REFORMATION

During the Reformation, the lands of the church were confiscated and transferred to the secular authorities. The peasants who lived on these lands and had a certain freedom to cultivate them, giving them a place in the world, were freed. Deprived of these lands, together with the collapse of feudalism, they became wage laborers. In this new status, they became abstract laborers without a significant place in the world politically. With the Reformation and secularization came the transition from feudalism to capitalism, which parallels what Arendt calls "the rise of the social."[8] All of these, of course, contributed to the intensification of world alienation.

CAPITALISM AND SECULARISM

By and large, the transition from feudalism to capitalism destroyed the stability and permanence of family and individual social structures into which pre-industrial European societies were organized. These were replaced by a "society" in which the accumulation of "social wealth" unleashed the "labor power" of the masses. What was liberated, really, is "the labor force" and "wage labor." The new laboring class which literally lived from hand to mouth stood not only directly under the compelling urgency of life's necessity—namely, a deep need to provide shelter, food, and ensuring their basic existence—but at the same time alienated from all cares and worries which did not immediately follow from the life process itself.

Alongside capitalism and the takeover of the social sphere over the private and public, Arendt indicates another factor in modern world alienation: secularization. But not in a theological context, as it is common to think of it; rather, she looks at this phenomenon in an innovative way—namely it is not that people suddenly lost their faith collectively. It is not turning one's back on

---

8. "The social" is related to the three events described here and to the last part of the present book in the discussion of the rise of the *animal laborans* and mass society.

God and the hereafter (the transcendent) and concentrating on "this world," but rather withdrawal into the self and world alienation. Modern man has not gained this world by losing the next.[9]

9. Arendt, *Human Condition*, 230.

CHAPTER 2

The Change in the Role of Science

THE DISCOVERY OF THE TELESCOPE

ARENDT CALLS THE THIRD event that she believes is at the beginning of the "modern age"[1] by several names: "Galileo's discovery of the telescope"; "the rise of modern science"; "the discovery of the Archimedean point." But they all mean the same thing. This telescope event caused a dramatic change in the role of science[2] and a "twofold flight from the earth."[3] Arendt's version of the history of modern science, which began with what is commonly called the "Revolution of Science," follows the lines of European and American thinkers in the field of physics and philosophy of science,[4] such as Erwin Schrödinger, Edwin Burtt, and Alexander Koyré,

1. I am following sections 36–37 in the last chapter of the book *The Human Condition*.

2. So much so that every science, not just physics and natural science, has changed its innermost content so radically that one may question whether there was any science at all before the modern age.

3. Arendt, *Human Condition*, 6.

4. Arendt clearly belongs to the humanities. Her engagement with discussions on natural science brought her out of her comfort zone. When she taught at Berkeley in 1955, she attended extended courses on physics. She also collected American and German press essays on a variety of scientific topics, such as astronomy, germ plasma, hydrogen fusion, and, after the launch of "Sputnik," the "space race." And immersed herself in the philosophy of science. All of these interests eventually shaped the book *The Human Condition*.

with whom she even met from time to time and corresponded regularly,[5] and the physicist Werner Heisenberg.[6]

According to Arendt, back in the cradle of Western thought in ancient Greece, man dreamed of being freed from the shackles of the earth. The most famous case is that of Archimedes of Syracuse, who claimed that if he got a fulcrum to place his lever on, he could move the earth from its place. This dream was finally realized by the harbingers of the scientific revolution, Galileo Galilei and René Descartes. Galileo's telescope was used as a lever that moved the earth from its old place at the center of the universe to its new place as a planet orbiting the sun. The fulcrum itself was the discovery of the moons of Jupiter—the first evidence of the existence of celestial bodies that do not orbit the earth, and hence the earth is not the center of all things.

In fact, the theoretical basis for the new universe model was laid before Galileo in the studies of Copernicus and Johannes Kepler. And even before that, Giordano Bruno and Nicolaus Cusanus had already made philosophical speculations about canceling the dichotomy between one earth and one sky above it. Their imagination challenged the finite, geocentric worldview that humans have held since time immemorial.[7] But despite their speculative

5. Her narrative of the history of science drew heavily from Koyré's *From the Closed World to the Infinite Universe* (1957). The similarities in the framework in which they approached the history of science can be seen in the opening pages of Koyré's book. During 1956 and 1957, Arendt began to read many of the works of early modern science and contemporary interpretations used by Koyré in his argument, taking notes in particular on Copernicus's *On the Revolutions of the Celestial Spheres* (1543), Johannes Kepler's *The New Astronomy* (1609), and Galileo's *The Starry Messenger* (1610).

6. To these should be added Alfred Whitehead, who influenced Arendt's development of the modern "process" idea, which will be discussed later. And finally, of course, the influence of Heidegger in general and his later reflections on technology in his famous essay "The Question Concerning Technology" (1954) are encapsulated in Arendt's writing. The issue of her fundamental disagreement with him has been sufficiently discussed elsewhere, and it does not belong to our discussion here.

7. Aristotle's theory, established in the fourth century BC, posited that the earth is the center of the world and everything above the moon is eternal. Astronomer Claudius Ptolemy contributed significantly to this theory. In 1543,

courage, Arendt argues that "in the field of ideas, there is only originality and depth, both of which are personal qualities, but not objective, complete innovation. Ideas come and go as distinguished from events; ideas are never unprecedented."[8]

The innovation in the event of the discovery of Galileo's telescope is therefore in revealing the secrets of the universe to human consciousness "with the certainty of sensory perception."[9] Galileo invited everyone to look through his telescope and see for themselves. By "confirming" the words of his predecessors, Galileo established the inspired speculations of his predecessors as a fact visible to everyone's eyes. According to Arendt, this event is equal in historical importance to the birth of Christ. And it led from here on to more important discoveries and technological development than the entire premodern period combined. And yet, at the time, this achievement remained the property of a minority of scientists who drew conclusions from it and founded in 1662 the "Society of Scientists and the Republic of the Spirit" (the Royal Society), which foreshadowed the radical cognitive change of all modern humans that only in our time (in the "modern world") became a visible political reality in which we all live in a world completely shaped by technology.

Polish astronomer Nicolaus Copernicus introduced a heliocentric model of the solar system in his treatise *On the Motion of the Heavenly Bodies* (*De revolutionibus orbium coelestium*). This model, which contradicted the traditional geocentric model, caused controversy with the religious establishment. Copernicus's theory influenced Galileo and the German astronomer Johannes Kepler, who accepted the heliocentric model. Kepler was the first to combine physics and astronomy, leading to the establishment of astrophysics.

8. Arendt, *Human Condition*, 235–36.

9. What sets Galileo apart from other heliocentric theorists is that he demonstrated that heliocentric theories were not only more useful devices for predicting data but also adequate descriptions of reality. Galileo himself emphasized this point: "Everyone can know with the certainty of sensory perception that the moon is in no way endowed with smooth and shining surfaces." Koyré, *From the Closed World*, 89.

GALILEO'S RELATIVISM

Although we are not standing at the point that Archimedes wanted but are bound to the earth probably forever, we have achieved the ability to act on the earth as if we had accessed it from the universe outside. This development became possible only after the dichotomy between heaven and earth was abolished and the universe became one. From now on, occurrences in nature are no longer seen as mundane but are subject to a "general cosmic law" that lies beyond the reach of our senses and the experience of the most superior devices, and even beyond the reach of human memory, the emergence of humanity, and the formation of the earth itself.[10]

Moreover, not only have we moved from the geocentric to the heliocentric model, but we have moved the Archimedean point one step to a point in the universe where even the sun is not at the center of a universal system. We move freely and choose a point of reference anywhere that suits a particular purpose we have determined. We have now become truly universal beings, living in a system of consciousness that has no fixed center. We are creatures who are mundane only by being alive but are able, by our choice, to overcome this condition, not merely in speculation but in practice. And on this, Arendt remarks that "the parentage of modern relativism is not in Einstein but in Galileo."[11] Arendt writes,

> Man hoped he could travel to the Archimedean point, which he found with the help of abstraction and imagination. But in doing so, once he physically reaches it after overcoming the limitations of nature, he will need another Archimedean point, *ad infinitum*. Man can only

10. Already with Galileo, certainly since Newton, the word "universal" began to have a very specific meaning, which is "valid beyond our solar system." And the meaning of the word "absolute" has changed as time, space, movement, or speed found in the universe compared to time, space, movement, or speed limited to the earth are only "relative." Everything that happens on earth becomes relative, since the universe becomes the point of reference for all measurements. Arendt, *Human Condition*, 245–46.

11. Arendt, *Human Condition*, 239.

get lost in the universe because the only true Archimedean point is the void behind the universe.[12]

The departure from the land symbolizes the release of the
limitations that nature gave us, and the deviation of the course of
the world represents man's ambition to direct nature as he wishes,
and in fact the "human condition" itself.

THE RISE OF MATHEMATICS AS A MODERN IDEAL

Along with the telescope event,[13] the Euclidean geometry that
dominated until then was replaced by algebra, thanks to which
mathematics "was able to free itself from the shackles of space,
that is, from the geometry, which, as its name indicates—the
measurement of the land—depends on earthly measures and
measurements."[14] Since it radically changed all the fields of science,
it is considered an "event" in itself. This new mental device allowed
the reduction of the data of the earthly senses and earthly movements to a mathematical language of symbols, through which it is
now possible to perceive dimensions and concepts that, until then,
were only perceived in a negative way because their size exceeds
human cognition.[15]

12. Arendt, *Between Past and Future*, 273.

13. Arendt placed more emphasis than Koyré on the role of the telescope
in aiding the rise of heliocentrism. Drawing on Burtt's claim in *The Metaphysical Foundations of Modern Science* (1932) that the influence of philosophers
such as Giordano Bruno was felt only after the telescope confirmed the claims
of their speculations, she argued that its invention and use led to the early
modern abandonment of geocentrism and constituted the "event of the modern age."

14. Burtt, *Metaphysical Foundations*, 44; Arendt, *Human Condition*, 240.

15. The rise of mathematics is not a result of Plato's belief that it was the
noblest of all sciences, second only to philosophy. The ideal forms of Plato
were given to the eyes of the spirit, like the data of the senses. Modernity has
led to the expansion of mathematics to the vast dimensions of an infinite universe, but it no longer focuses on phenomena. Instead, it becomes a science of
the structure of human consciousness. Phenomena can only be saved to the
extent that they can be reduced to a mathematical order. This mathematical
operation does not prepare human cognition for the revelation of a real being

The possibility to discuss "things that exist" but cannot be "seen" with the mind's eye opened the door to a new way of meeting nature within the framework of the "experiment," which was a modern innovation in itself. Instead of observing natural phenomena as given,[16] moderns subordinate nature to the conditions of human cognition—that is, conditions obtained from a universal astrophysical point of view found in the universe.

THE TREND OF INTERNALIZATION OF THE SCIENCE OF THE ARCHIMEDEAN POINT

We began to rely not on our senses to understand the world but on tools. We started building devices to prepare experiments, and what we see in the world is not the world as it is, but things that are seen through devices and experiments that we built ourselves—that is, contain all our biases and prejudices.[17] According to Arendt, this is the trend of internalization that characterizes "universal science." We began to see the world not objectively but through our rational attempt to understand it. And this is what Arendt calls "modern relativism." We begin to enter into ourselves and see not the world as such, but ourselves—namely, the world as we have created it.[18]

---

by directing it to the ideal dimensions appearing in the data conveyed by the senses. Instead, it reduces these data to the degree of human consciousness, allowing it to observe the multiplicity and diversity of concrete and treat it according to its own patterns and symbols.

16. The Greeks believed in providing "proofs" of phenomena through thought and logical deductions, such as Aristotle's proof of vacuum existence. The modern turning point in scientific thinking was the development of the trial-and-error model, with Galileo and Kepler being practical.

17. The Galilean method's radical disregard for sensual and material reality promised to transfer the secrets of the universe to recognition "with the certainty of sensory perception." These changes in thought were accompanied by experimental practices that established conditions of human thought for natural processes and forced them to fall into man-made patterns and recreated them in the laboratory.

18. As mentioned, this leads to optimism—we can actually produce the world according to our image and likeness. We become almost gods. On the other hand, it leads to despair; since we are limited to what we can produce, we

"UNIVERSAL" SCIENCE AND THE TRANSITION TO THE "MODERN WORLD"

This change in the transition from Aristotelian concepts of nature (geophysics) to a science in which the universe became a reference point for all measurements (astrophysics that began with Galileo)—that is, mechanistic and mathematical hypotheses based on the methods of experimental science—was the first stage of modern science in the older part of modernity that Arendt calls the "modern age." Its goal was to gain better control over the earth.

However, what separates the "modern age" in which people already knew that the earth revolves around the sun, from the "modern world" in which we live today, is the difference between a science that observes nature from a universal point of view and thus achieves full control over it, and a truly "universal" science that imports cosmic processes into nature, even at the obvious risk that this would destroy it.[19] The meaning of "action into nature" is a transition from "natural" science—from Aristotle's tradition of wonder and awe toward nature (Greek: *thaumazein*)—back (chronologically) to Archimedes—that is, to a new science that is no longer concerned with classifying phenomena but with (re) creating them in laboratory conditions, which requires action "within" the conditions of their possibility.[20]

---

are stuck in a world of human production, and there is nothing beyond that.

19. In the context of the discourse on the Anthropocene, the moderns have turned from the agents of history into one of many life processes on earth. Their interpolation into nature, for example, the injection of "new material," or human action, into geological strata, can actually be seen as turning man into a geo-natural force.

20. In the context of the history of science, there is a transition from the "wonder" approach of Aristotelian science, which notices and classifies phenomena in the world as they are, i.e., a passive science that respects the nature given to us, to an "active and working" science that strives to change nature and recreate it according to the needs and goals of man. This claim is similar to Heidegger's critique of modern science and technology. According to him, there is no *poetry* in modern technology. Instead, there is a challenging (German: *Herausfordern*) of nature in an irrational demand to produce energy that we can store (Heidegger, *Question Concerning Technology*, 14); that is, to challenge in the negative sense of coercion by force, like strangling someone

The new creative power makes it possible to produce new elements that have never been found in nature—for example, new celestial bodies in the form of satellites, to turn mass into energy, and perhaps in the near future, to reproduce the miracle of life.[21] We have occupied the place that, until modern times, was reserved for God alone.[22] We have found the means to create processes of cosmic origin—for example, to introduce nanoparticles into the earth and change it. There are companies that plan to build new planets in space.[23] They will be partly technological and partly natural. In short, spaceships, satellites, and space stations all express an attempt to rethink what it means to not only control nature but to create a cosmologically new kind of a world.

As mentioned, it took two hundred years until this new science of the Archimedean point developed its full potential and the moderns began to truly live in a world that was literally shaped by science and technology.[24] According to Arendt, historically, this

---

in the hope that he will overcome it, as if we are telling him, We hope you can breathe. According to Heidegger, modern science and technology challenge nature to "submit" and provide energy to be captured, stored, pass a quality check, and mean something. For example, a coal mine: in modern eyes, the mine reveals itself as a coal mining area and the earth as a deposit of minerals, which is a different approach from premodern forms. A wind farm, for example, releases energy from the air but allows the wind to be what it is. Heidegger, *Question Concerning Technology*, 15–18.

21. Arendt, *Human Condition*, 244–45.

22. Arendt uses the word "to create" deliberately, to indicate that we are actually doing what all ages before ours thought to be reserved only for God. Arendt, *Human Condition*, 245.

23. For example, Jeff Bezos's vision of building giant space stations with normal earth gravity as a solution for overpopulation on earth. According to Bezos, we undoubtedly live better than in past times, medically-wise, etc., and we want to use more energy with right. The only thing that moves backwards is the condition of nature. As an advanced society, we better move to space to establish colonies so we may use even more energy—for instance, extract materials from the moon and nearby planets. And maybe move the heavy industry to space too, in order to slow the destruction of nature. According to Bezos, the time to do it is arguable, but it should be done for certain. See Bezos, "Human Population."

24. Arendt, *Human Condition*, 247.

"modern world" was born in the twentieth century with the first atomic explosion experiments.[25]

DESPAIR AND VICTORY: GAINING CONTROL AT THE COST OF LOSING REALITY

Galileo's innovation brought with it a sense of supreme victory that we had fulfilled Archimedes's wish by finding a point outside the earth from which we could disconnect it and force it to finally reveal the secrets of nature. We are able to perceive and know everything—the moon, space moons, black holes, cell shapes, creating new humans, and building new worlds. That's the optimistic side.[26] On the other hand, modern astrophysics, that began with Galileo, left us with a universe of which all we know is the way its properties affect our measuring instruments. Instead of objective knowledge of the world as it is, we find instrument data.

The phrase that best captures this situation, according to Arendt, is Heisenberg's formulation: "Man confronts himself alone."[27] In fact, the rise of "experiments" for the purpose of gain-

---

25. Arendt, *Human Condition*, 6. According to Arendt, the "modern age" is an age of science and the internalization of the world, and the discovery of the telescope defined it. But it remained only an elitist discourse. The "modern world" first started with the dropping of the atomic bomb on Hiroshima and the landing on the moon, and then it started to have a sweeping effect on everyone in the world.

26. The moderns understood what Archimedes understood: the metaphor of the Archimedean point means, Give me a point far enough away from it and I can move it out of place; that is, the secrets of nature can only be discovered from outside of it.

27. Heisenberg indicates, "If so, what is the existential change brought about by science? Well, that man meets only himself and has no partners or opponents. In the past, man met only with nature. He had to look at all kinds of creatures in nature. Today, man meets only things he created himself." Heisenberg, *Conception of Nature*, 2. The point of Heisenberg's claim is that the object of observation has no existence independent of the observing subject: "Through the art of observation, it will be decided which direction will be set for the course of nature and which direction will be erased through our own observation." Heisenberg, *Wandlungen in den Grundlagen*, 67.

ing knowledge was already the result of the belief that humans can only know what they have done themselves.

To summarize, this event confronted man with a difficult decision: that the most terrible old fear—that our senses, the organs through which we perceive reality, might betray us—and the most presumptuous hope of human speculative thought—the Archimedean wish for a point outside the earth from which we can disconnect it—come in one package. Only if we lose reality and the fear is fully realized will we receive as compensation control over heavenly forces.[28]

28. Arendt, *Human Condition*, 237–38.

CHAPTER 3

The Dilemmas of Modern
Philosophy in Face
of the Loss of Certainty

THE UNIVERSAL DOUBT

THE OTHER IMPORTANT FIGURE next to Galileo in the revolution of modernity was René Descartes. According to Arendt, the discoveries of science had a decisive influence on modern philosophy that began with Descartes, to the point of changing its internal content and function. For Arendt, Descartes actually completed Galileo's move.[1]

Arendt opens with an historical argument: modern philosophy began with the doubt of Descartes. This doubt is not skepticism or self-criticism, but universal, which makes it more radical than Galileo's because it encompasses all areas of life. No thought or experience will escape it, even religion. It became a cultural norm just as Aristotelian wonder was central to premodern culture. The advantage of reason over the senses is no longer relevant here because truth and reality are not given to us as they are.

The two major texts that Galileo composed on the telescope when he first started using it were on his observations of the moons of Saturn and on the mountains on our moon. When we look at

---

1. I am following section 38 in the last part of *The Human Condition.*

the moon, we notice bright spots and dark spots. Galileo assumed that the dark points were shadows. And if there are shadows, there must be mountains. Considering the angle of the sun's illumination of the moon, the height of these mountains can be calculated. Indeed, two hundred years later, it turned out that he was right. But the point is that he didn't see any "mountains," but shadows and lights. In other words, Arendt claims, what Galileo really taught is that through the telescope, it is proven that the perception of the senses is unreliable and that the real way to obtain knowledge is mathematics.[2] Like Galileo, Descartes was also a mathematician, and he too believed that truth could only be achieved mathematically.[3] Galileo's Archimedean point confirmed his great concern with our reliance on our senses for the determination of philosophical or scientific truths.

THE LOSS OF CERTAINTY

Descartes was haunted by two nightmares, which became the nightmares of the entire modern age. In one of them, what we see as "reality" may be nothing but a dream. The other nightmare concerns the human condition as a whole, as revealed in the new

2. In a series of observations in 1610, he discovered, among other things, that the surface of the moon is not smooth, that the planet Jupiter is surrounded by four moons, and that there are spots on the sun. These discoveries showed that the heliocentric model was possible. Kepler defended Galileo's findings. In any case, Arendt wants to say that only Galileo's observations of the planet Venus with the help of the telescope he built were the first real evidence of Copernicus's theory.

3. Inspired by Galileo, Descartes developed the analytic geometry that placed engineering bodies within what has since been called the "Cartesian coordinate system." The strength of analytic geometry lies in its ability to use theorems and algebraic calculations to solve geometric problems. This new tool was later used by Gottfried von Leibniz and Isaac Newton to discover differential and integral calculus, which provided the mathematical basis for modern physics. It is true that the axis system resides in an infinite space without a center, similar to the new model of the universe born as a result of Galileo's discoveries, but in order to use it to perform calculations, an Archimedean point must be determined—the origin of the axes. This is done by the axis users as they see fit, according to the needs of the specific calculation.

discoveries and the idea that man cannot trust his senses and reason. In these circumstances, there is a possibility that an evil spirit, a deceptive demon, betrays us willingly and maliciously. The height of the wickedness of that malevolent spirit would be to create a human being endowed with the concept of truth only to endow him with faculties by means of which he could never arrive at any truth and never be able to know anything with certainty.

Indeed, what has been lost in the modern age is certainty—and more than that.

DOUBT IN LOGIC

Although the Cartesian doubt came in response to Galileo's discoveries through the telescope, it is, as mentioned, more radical than doubting the reliability of the senses because it led to the abandonment of "appearance" and its relationship to truth[4] and also to the abandonment of logic[5] and even faith. It is a universal doubt that has invaded every field, even religion (Kierkegaard[6]). We have lost faith not only in the senses but in any kind of rationality. We doubt everything. Descartes's nightmare has come true: reality can only be a dream, and there may be no "truth." When I talk about objects outside my window, I'm not talking about them but about my mind, with which I can play with them and reduce things. But nothing will tell me anything about the world in itself.

In conclusion, modern philosophy began with the doubt of Descartes, but not as a self-correct organ inherent in human consciousness against the deceptions of thought and the illusions of the senses, against prejudices, or for criticism in scientific

---

4. Everything must be questioned until being and appearance are separated forever. Plato, an idealist, had an idea. And there's the appearance. They are simultaneously separated and linked, whereas in the modern age, this connection has been questioned. For instance, consider Kant's "thing in itself." Its presumption is that we have no access to the thing itself, only impressions of it in our consciousness.

5. Since we doubt our senses, we also doubt our logic, and we are left only with our mental processes, which can be reliable or not, but not right or wrong.

6. Kierkegaard, *Philosophical Fragments*.

investigation. This is a doubt, which doubts that truth exists at all. It doubts everything (*dubitandum omnibus de est*).

INTROSPECTION

Descartes sought to overcome the despair of being thrown into a radically contingent world due to the discovery of the telescope, and the solution he found was to move the locus of certainty from the transcendental to the interior in the form of a rational subject—namely, replacing the Archimedean point that is somewhere in the universe with a subjective but certain point of reference: "I think therefore I exist" with certainty.[7] From the very logical certainty that when I doubt something, I remain aware of the process of casting doubt in my consciousness, Descartes concluded that those processes that take place in a person's own mind have their own certainties, which can be made the object of inquiry by introspection.[8] Now that the reference point is in the human mind, we can create universal mathematical-algebraic formulas that will work with some certainty wherever we go, even though our senses are unreliable. As mentioned, Descartes completed Galileo's move. After escaping from the earth to a point in the universe, introspection marks the appearance of what Arendt calls the "twofold alienation" in the withdrawal from the world into the self.

MOVING FROM "TRUTH" TO TRUTHFULNESS AND FINALLY TO "CERTAINTY"

The meaning of introspection, moving the point of reference from the universe to subjective individual certainty that something exists, is that, since Descartes, the interest of modern philosophy is not truth or reality but reliability as a type of certainty. This

7. To Galileo's new understanding of man's place in the universe, Descartes attached this solipsistic form of subjectivism through an analytic geometry based on the possibility of taking an extraterrestrial epistemological position. The result was the placement of the Archimedean point inside the self.

8. Arendt, *Human Condition*, 254–316.

credibility is achieved by the fact that the person knows what he has created by himself. From now on, the scientific objectivity that is based on process and procedure is not designed for finding truth but for a kind of reliability. Namely, if we do this and that, we will get a known result that can be trusted.

MAN KNOWS ONLY WHAT HE HIMSELF HAS CREATED

If Descartes's entire move is based on the fact that the intellect can only know what it has created and that it holds within itself, it is found that not only the scientists meet only themselves (as Heisenberg said), but also the philosophers. Although truth cannot be known as something visible and given, at least man can know what he has done himself. Descartes' solution to the problem of certainty echoes what the scientists discovered; namely, even if there is no truth, man can be a truth teller.[9] Hence, again, the supreme ideal of this must be mathematical knowledge—that is, knowledge that does not need the sensual confirmation of reality. This has become the prevailing approach in the modern age. We only know what we have created ourselves, and thus the world becomes a fabricated product of our rational mind.

LOSS OF COMMON SENSE

The trend of internalization in the scientific revolution also occurs in the field of philosophy. All modern thought leads man deep into himself and contentment with a reliable consciousness of the world instead of the world as it is.[10] The problem is that introspection has caused the common sense, which used to connect people's five senses to a common world, to become an internal capacity with no relation to the world we are supposed to share together. What

9. Arendt, *Human Condition*, 315.

10. As a result, modern morality is no longer based on a real standard but on reliability and outcome.

remains common to humans is the structure of their brains—that is, the overwhelming consensus that two plus two equals four. And this can be expanded *ad infinitum* within the brain without real results in the world. Moreover, it is even convincing because the brain structure of all human beings is the same. In other words, "reason" for Descartes (and Hobbes) became "reckoning with consequences"[11] a capacity for deduction that man can release within himself at any given moment. But it is not something that is shared, like a common world. When man is deprived of the common sense that connects the rest of his senses to the world shared with other human beings, he is reduced to the rank of an animal capable of "reckoning with consequences."[12]

---

11. Arendt, *Human Condition*, 257.

12. Arendt, *Human Condition*, 295. Our thinking has moved from terms of right and wrong to "cash for calculation." We have become animals that are able to reason.

CHAPTER 4

The Modern Worldview

ARENDT THUS CONNECTS THE two great events—the discovery of the telescope and the modern philosophy that developed from it—in order to draw the profile of modern mentality that emerged from it.[1] Because of Descartes's introspection, man carries the Archimedean point wherever he goes, which means complete liberation from the "human condition" of being an earthly creature. But this liberty does not seem more convincing than the universal doubt it was trying to overcome. Despite the certainty that Descartes offers us, the overall implication of this is still uncertain. There will always be a suspicion that this world we have built in our consciousness is just a dream.

THE CRISIS OF NATURAL SCIENCE

In the previous section, we saw that the changes due to the revolution of science and philosophy required mathematical innovations that made it possible to present non-sensory standards and measurements to the human mind as if they were sense data. The "mathematization of science"—in an accordance with Descartes's introspection—reduced sensory data and worldly phenomena to the "measures of the human mind." But this is not really possible

1. I am following section 40 in the last part of *The Human Condition*.

because, through mathematics, we can produce equations, shapes, and designs beyond our intellect—for example, a round triangle.[2]

Arendt reminds us that non-Euclidean systems of mathematics were discovered without the intention of applying them empirically. Only later did they receive surprising validity in Einstein's theory. The fear is that the application is possible even to the most distant pure mathematical structures. For example, if new universes suddenly emerge that "prove" every all-encompassing pattern that the mind has come up with, then seemingly we can celebrate the "harmony" we hoped for between mathematics and physics, spirit and matter, man and universe.

The suspicion that the world we invented in our consciousness is only a dream will only increase when we discover that happenings in the micro (atom) obey the same laws and order as in the macro (planets).[3] Thus, from an astronomical point of view on nature, we get planetary systems. Conversely, astronomical investigations from a terrestrial perspective will show terrestrial geocentric systems. But the truth is that every time we try to go beyond the phenomena and reach an experience beyond the reach of the senses—even with accurate devices—in order to capture the secrets of Being, we see that the same patterns dominate the micro and macro. And so, we will be disappointed again that the "unity of the universe" we have found has nothing to do with micro and macro but with the patterns of our cognition, the same cognition that designed the devices and subjected nature to the conditions of our experiments. We dictate to nature its laws, and what is this if not Descartes's nightmare about a deceiving demon inside our minds, mocking our thirst for knowledge? According to Arendt,

2. For this analysis, Arendt relied on Edwin Burtt (Burtt, *Metaphysical Foundations*, 63). Today's AI software is one illustration of this, as it can generate visuals and shapes that are beyond human comprehension.

3. Arendt refers here to Heisenberg's claim that the incompatibilities between logic and reality are manifested in the fact that the electrons, which are supposed to explain the sensory properties of matter, themselves lack such properties. Heisenberg, *Wandlungen in den Grundlagen*, 66. To this Arendt adds that the scientists finally realized that if a substance has no properties, it can no longer be called "matter."

this is a vicious circle. The scientists formulate their hypotheses, organize their experiments, and use these experiments to verify the hypotheses. Therefore, this whole enterprise is hypothetical. As long as we do science through experiments, we do not encounter the real world, but only in the way we have organized it in our theories.[4] And so, with the rise of science and the new internalization of thought that goes along with it (passing the Archimedean point into our mind), we replace the given sensory world with a scientific truth about the world.[5] This embarrassment is expressed today in the "modern world." Despite their achievements, scientists are haunted by the same nightmares as Descartes at the beginning of the modern age. We perceive the world abstractly with a mind that observes it from an Archimedean point outside the senses and the world. Mathematics can produce shapes and designs that have not been seen in the world.

SCIENCE AND TECHNOLOGY

And so, science uses technology to "prove" that it deals with an "authentic" order in nature.[6] The answers to the questions presented in the experiments are obtained in invisible mathematical terms. Yet technology shows that the truth of the most abstract concepts of modern science can be applied with results:

---

4. Arendt, *Human Condition*, 261. Arendt quotes Max Planck here: "The creator of a hypothesis enjoys unlimited possibilities and is also almost not bound by the functioning of his organs and senses or the instruments he uses. . . . It can also be said that he creates geometry in the form of his fantasy; therefore, measurements can never directly confirm or refute hypotheses. They can only highlight the least or greatest fit." Weil, "Réflexions," 102–19.

5. As Heisenberg indicated, "the mathematical formula no longer describes nature as it is, but rather our knowledge of it (as in quantum theory). In modern atomic physics, we have accepted this situation because it describes our experiment adequately; that is, it is not what the scientific truth was in the past—the description of nature as it is. And this is the symptom of the crisis we are in." Heisenberg, *Conception of Nature*, 25.

6. Heisenberg, *Wandlungen in den Grundlagen*, 64.

The sad truth of the matter, is that the lost contact between the world of the senses and appearances and the physical world view has been re-established not by the pure scientist but by the "plumber." The technicians, who account today for the overwhelming majority of all "researchers," have brought the results of the scientists down to earth . . . even though the scientist is still beset by paradoxes . . . the very fact that whole technology could be developed from his results demonstrates the "soundness" of his theories and hypotheses more convincingly than any merely scientific observation or experiment ever could.[7]

THE SEPARATION OF THOUGHT FROM SENSORY EXPERIENCE

The implication of the mathematization of physics is that man can do things without understanding them. "Our brain, which constitutes the physical, material condition of our thoughts, is unable to follow what we do, so that from now on we would indeed need artificial machines to do our thinking and speaking."[8] The formulas are not things. We have never seen a vacuum or atoms. They are based on mere calculations. But for us, their formula is "correct." And so, we care more about the theory than the senses.[9]

Arendt did not mention it, but Heisenberg described this mindset also through a parable:

7. Arendt, *Between Past and Future*, 268.

8. Arendt, *Human Condition*, 4. It can be said that Arendt anticipated here the current debate around the consequences of the transition to the use of "thinking machines" (AI), on society—for example, the future of creativity, human memory, criticality, etc.

9. For example, nuclear fusion, which is similar to the process that occurs in the sun (the source of its energy), is a process that requires enormous temperatures. The extraction of the melting energy is, of course, a very big promise, thanks to the economic advantage. However, the difficulty is in finding a facility where it is possible to generate the same tremendous temperature needed to fuse hydrogen nuclei, a temperature that will melt any possible tool. Meaning that the knowledge is here, but technically it is impossible.

> Our position is analogous to a captain whose ship has been built so strongly of steel and iron that the magnetic needle of its compass no longer responds to anything but the iron structures of the ship. It no longer points north. The ship can no longer be steered to reach any goal.[10]

This topic is related to Arendt's insight from her last unfinished book, *The Life of the Mind*, that all thinking must be based on the senses. We cannot think outside of language, for example, about a unicorn. And the language draws its metaphors from reality that everyone perceives in common sense.[11] Although the "truths" of modern science are presented in mathematical formulas and "proved" through technology, they are no longer available for speech and thought. Any attempt to formulate them conceptually and coherently fails. Arendt quotes Schrödinger: "It comes out perhaps not as a 'triangular circle' but much more so than a 'winged tiger.'"[12] It becomes clear to us that nature behaves differently from what we know from the sense of sight, until no sense-based model can be correct. The situation that science has created has great political importance, because where speech is the focus, things become political by definition. Speech turns man into a political creature.

If we surrender to the authority of science, then we have essentially adopted an anti-political way of life in which speech is no longer significant because the language of mathematical signs contains statements that cannot be translated back into ordinary speech. The meaning of the separation between thought and the sensory experience inherent in the "human condition" is that, with the loss of reality, the transcendent is also lost—namely, our ability to review in a conceptual way that is understandable within the framework of our reason. By losing the sensory world, we also lose the world of truth, the ideals. There is only the world that man has created.

---

10. Heisenberg, *Conception of Nature*, 30.

11. Arendt, *Life of the Mind*, 103.

12. Arendt, *Human Condition*, 3.

To summarize, Arendt writes that "the scientist is capable of doing more than he is capable of understanding."[13] In this climate, many of us moderns toy with the powers of contemporary technology and are able to do things without understanding. "It simply works."[14]

THE DECLINE OF PHILOSOPHY AND THE STRENGTHENING OF SCIENCE

Since the seventeenth century, philosophy has produced excellent results when it investigated, through introspection, the processes of the senses and the mind. In this sense, most modern philosophy is indeed a theory of cognition and psychology (as in Pascal, Kierkegaard, and Nietzsche)—namely, a study of material processes in the brain that is mainly concerned with the question of what can be known. But, despite their brilliant achievements, the status of the philosophers has declined unprecedentedly. In the Middle Ages philosophy was a second fiddle (the slave of theology), but modern philosophy has been relegated to third-fiddle status. According to Arendt, after Descartes based his philosophy on the discoveries of Galileo, philosophy has always remained one step behind the scientists and their increasingly amazing discoveries, whose principles philosophy strives to discover *ex post facto* and adapt to a comprehensive introspection of nature and human knowledge.

As such, philosophy is unnecessary for the scientists, who do not need a slave.[15] The philosophers became epistemologists who take care of the general theory of science, which the scientists

13. Arendt, *Between Past and Future*, 273.

14. Arendt's point is that knowledge and thought are separated in the sense that we are unable to think rationally about what we are doing. We have become slaves to technology and computing, not in the sense that the machine will dominate us as certain futurists think, but in the sense that technology speaks in a language reserved for experts and is not understood by the common sense of ordinary people. We board a flight without having the faintest idea how an airplane works. This language replaced the language that allowed us to tell stories about the world we share together.

15. Arendt, *Human Condition*, 267.

themselves do not need; that is, the philosophers pursue the scientists in an attempt to understand what they are doing. But they try to understand what happened even without them.

In the context of the discussion on this supremacy and autonomy of modern science, Arendt elaborates on the subject of the Royal Society mentioned in the previous section, and adds a very important point related to her entire thesis on the relationship between science and politics in modernity. Allegedly, the members of this organization pledged to the king not to interfere in any discourse—religious, political, or otherwise—except for science, which gave rise to the modern scientific ideal of "objectivity." But according to Arendt, this ideal cannot be non-political, because scientific teamwork cannot be pure science, but rather a desire for power, like in any organization. Since its beginning, this institution became a moral center of influence that dictated the new standards of judgment. For example, instead of a spring-like view of an observer of nature, now comes the question of the success of the experiment: will it work or not? The theory became a hypothesis, and the hypothesis became "truth." As mentioned, the truth was converted into credibility, which is a self-lie. And so, instead of acting from the networks of human relationships inherent in the world, which is how authentic political action is achieved, the collective effort of scientists to capture the secrets of nature through experiments took on the alienated position of a universal science operating in the world and on earth, which is formulated in a mathematical language that isolates their actions in an opaque language and has gained enormous political power since. In fact, it has become an epistemic authority that strives to dictate the rules of politics and society.[16]

This leads us to the next section and the discussion on the elimination of contemplation. When reality is not waiting for us to discover it, there is nothing to contemplate anymore.

16. Arendt, *Human Condition*, ch. 6, note 26.

CHAPTER 5

The Human Condition in Modernity

IN THIS SECTION,[1] I will explain how everything we have discussed so far is reflected in terms of Arendt's conceptualization (phenomenology) of human activities, namely a sequence of events in the category of "active life" of man that resulted from the three events that brought about modernity: the study of the planet, the deprivation of the land and capitalism, and the changes in the role of science and philosophy that resulted from the telescope. In other words, Arendt shows the political meaning of all this.[2]

---

1. I am following sections 41–42 in the last chapter of *The Human Condition*.

2. Arendt's unorthodox intellectual approach is indeed the source of her originality. But it dragged her more than once into problems. Although she did not see herself as being limited to a certain category or academic catalogs, Arendt clearly belongs to the humanities. Thus, I am afraid that in her historical investigation in our discussions here, which she claims is designed to trace the origins of modern alienation from the world (Arendt, *Human Condition*, 5–6), she makes transitions between exact sciences, historical events, and ideas that might not seem convincing in the eyes of contemporary mainstream historians. For example, she does not consider the extent of Vico's influence—namely, how many of his books were printed, how many understood them, and so on. Although history was not considered empirical in the early modern age, today it is; for example, in the works of Michel Foucault and Francis Fukuyama who, like Arendt, tried to explain historical events with the help of their own conceptual model and also supported their arguments with loads of factual details.

THE RISE OF "ACTIVE LIFE"

The mental implication of the discovery of the Archimedean point and the corresponding rise of Cartesian doubt was the reversal of the hierarchical order between the "life of contemplation" and the "active life" in the seventeenth century.[3] However, it is not just a simple reversal of the hierarchical order between contemplation and doing because contemplation, in the original sense of observing the truth, is completely eliminated.[4] The reversal here concerns only the relationship between thinking and doing; that is, thinking and contemplation are not the same. Thinking, which was traditionally seen as the most important and direct way that leads to the study of truth[5]—in fact, it was the slave of contemplation—has now become the slave of action.[6]

The connection of the exchange of contemplation with action to Galileo is clear. The fact that he made the discoveries using a telescope, a product of human craft (*work*), indicates an important change in science, namely that knowledge is acquired not only by thinking but by doing.

After being and appearance have separated and truth is no longer supposed to appear, i.e., reveal itself to the mental eye of the observer, a necessity arises to hunt for the truth behind deceptive appearances. And for the task of obtaining reliable knowledge, contemplation as passive observation becomes meaningless. It is better to rely on doing rather than contemplation because it is the telescope device that finally forced nature, and the universe, to reveal their secrets. Henceforth, truth and knowledge can only be obtained through "action" and not through contemplation. What's more, technology wouldn't have developed if it didn't rely on practicality. In the previous section, we saw that certain knowledge can only be obtained if it is related to what man has made himself, and

3. Arendt, *Human Condition*, 262.

4. I will elaborate on the specific factors that made the contemplation meaningless, mainly the penetration of the "process" idea into action, in the next chapter.

5. Arendt, *Human Condition*, 264.

6. Arendt, *Human Condition*, 265.

therefore its ideal has become mathematical knowledge[7] where we deal with entities that man has made himself in his mind.

Now let's rephrase that: In order to be certain, we need to "verify"—that is, subject the world to our experiments. And in order to "know," we have to do. From now on, the nature of knowledge is such that it can only be tested through more doing.[8]

As we shall see immediately, the type of action that defined this rise of "active life" to the top of the order of priorities is not the political action that Arendt values from antiquity in the Greek polis. Historically, the first reversal was from action in ancient times to contemplation in the Middle Ages. The transition from the Middle Ages to the modern age was characterized by the reversal of contemplation to *homo faber* rather than action.

THE VICTORY OF THE *HOMO FABER*

The next reversal took place within "active life" itself. The action, which, as mentioned, took the place of reference, was changed to "making." Instruments led to the modern revolution; thus, it is conceivable that the prestige of the *homo faber* model rose with the Industrial Revolution to the status of a common sense, a cultural norm. What we do as modern humans is make things. But *homo faber* was upgraded not only because he was a tool maker but also because he helped in obtaining scientific knowledge. After all, the modern experiment, the new model of scientific investigation,

---

7. Arendt, *Human Condition*, 263.

8. As Heisenberg put it, "I work to understand." Heisenberg, *Conception of Nature*, 66. According to Arendt, the fundamental experience of the modern age is that truth and knowledge depend on man and what he says. And so the telescope, as an instrument and not our senses, provides us with truth and certainty. And not because it enhances our sense of the magnifying lens, but because it allows us to apply theories through experiments to the world and believe that we control the world. In this sense, in order to be sure, we have to make sure—that is, to subject the world to our experiments. Thus, we are again moving away from the world of things, from our senses, from the truth, and from ourselves. And all this is because of the rise of action instead of contemplation.

produces for itself the results it is interested in and is therefore dependent on human productive capacity.[9] In the previous chapter, I mentioned that the "life of contemplation" was pushed to the bottom of the list of priorities. I will immediately explain the particular reason that the philosopher was relegated to the position of a bystander, one who can only wonder about what the scientists have shown.

In any case, *homo faber* is the modern guide. From now on, all scientific and technological progress depends on instruments. Discoveries in the nineteenth century were achieved on the merit of new technological developments, and so they could not have happened before.

Indeed, the *homo faber* mentality is reflected in the salient features of the modern age whose ideals are productivity and creativity—namely, the instrumentalization of the world; his confidence in devices; his reliance on the means-ends category; his belief that every problem can be solved and that every human motivation has been reduced to usefulness; a sovereignty that treats everything given as matter; his view of all nature as a huge factory from which he can cut what he wants; his contempt for all thought that cannot be considered to be "the first step to the fabrication of artificial objects, particularly of tools to make tools, and to vary their fabrication indefinitely."[10] But the crucial point here is, as mentioned, his self-evident identification between production and action.[11]

MIXING ACTION AND KNOWLEDGE

In the discussion on the changing role of science, we saw that the use of experimentation is the expression of the belief that man can only know what he has done himself. The experiment repeats natural processes in the laboratory with the aim of reproducing them. As Kant said, "Give me matter, and I will show you how

9. Arendt, *Human Condition*, 268.

10. Arendt, *Human Condition*, 279.

11. Arendt, *Human Condition*, 279.

a world develops from it."[12] According to Arendt, this formulation captures the essence of modern mixing between doing and knowing. Experiencing the knowledge of the way of doing is an apprenticeship to train a person to do what he wants to know. The consequence of this concept is the change of emphasis in the history of science from the traditional question of "what" the thing itself is to the question of "how" it came into being (its creation process). The answer to which can only be obtained, as mentioned, in an experiment in which natural processes are repeated from a divine position of the re-creation of nature.

THE "PROCESSES"

The ideals of modernity correspond to the characteristics of *homo faber*. But according to Arendt, there is a more significant element in the transition from the question "what" the thing is to "how" it was created—namely, that the subject of science is no longer nature or the universe, but history. The moderns do not ask, for example, what a bridge is, but how and by what processes it comes into being and how it can be reproduced.[13]

This idea of a further development of the modern man's mentality runs through all of Arendt's writings in the late fifties and early sixties and is one of her most important and topical. There are several reasons for the appearance of the concept of "process."

1. From that difficult state of modern thought due to the discovery of the telescope and the Cartesian doubt, in which logic is no longer an inner light that reveals truth and has become an ability to "calculate with results," modern man began to test his abilities for action. If man is the measure of everything, and he can only understand with certainty what he has made

12. Kant, "Universal Natural History," 200.

13. Unlike the attempt behind the ancient conception of immortality, in which man created things from material from the natural environment, the attempt behind the modern conception of the process arose precisely from the despair of nature.

himself, then why won't he build reality himself—namely, the nature that has always limited him, and even human history—like a craft product, and thus he will be able to control his destiny.

2. An unprecedented development of modern historical consciousness. In her article "The Concept of History" (1958)[14] Arendt contrasts two ideas of history: ancient and modern. For the Greeks and Romans, nature was seen as immortal, found in an eternal circle of existence—for example, the stars in the sky. And man is finite, and thus his existence is meaningless. In this ancient concept, the emphasis is on unusual single events that break the flow of time, such as people's extraordinary deeds and creations. The task of the historian and the poet was to document them so that they would always be remembered and hence to grant them immortality. Thus, in the ancient concept, history accepts into its pantheon, which exists in the immortal dimension, mortal human individuals and objects that have proven to be equal to nature. And this is the meaning of their glory.

This concept has changed in the modern age due to the loss of faith in the idea of the immortality of nature and man. The moderns no longer attach special significance to single events that deserve to be remembered.

The background for the penetration of the experimental mode of investigation into historical understanding was also the growing tendency to see the earth from an Archimedean point of view that regards the natural and human worlds as a unified field subject to the same laws and part of the same story. From now on, nature and human history are seen as two processes that make up a single, all-encompassing metanarrative. From the absence of boundaries between nature and humanity, the view was born that what can be done in history can also be done in the natural realm.[15] Natural pro-

14. Arendt, *Between Past and Future*, 41–90.

15. Arendt's radicalization of Whitehead's description of nature as a process was related to her epochal claims about the relationship between politics

cesses can be started by humans and vice versa, man "acts into history" as if history consisted of phenomena suitable for experiment.[16]

Within this vast metanarrative, nature and history were condemned to endless progress without reaching any structured telos or approaching any predetermined idea. The meaning of events ceased to be valued in their individuality but in their role of service to that metanarrative whose value is measured by utility, means and ends, something through which we want to achieve our goals. Thus, due to the loss of faith in the modern age in the idea of immortality, nature is no longer static or immortal, but something that human action (processes) can affect. While for the Greeks, the Romans, and the ancient idea of history, human actions were opposed

---

and technology and nature and history. During the modern age, she claims, man sought to "act into history" as if history consisted of phenomena suitable for experiment. The twentieth century also saw a qualitative change in the view that what can be done in history can also be done in the natural realm. However, while the totalitarians wrongly defined freedom as the ability to intervene in the apparently natural or quasi-natural processes that shape humanity, nuclear physics threatened to break the world, essentially starting cosmic and natural processes and worlds within the natural realm. This, Arendt argued, was the hallmark of the atomic age.

16. In this context Arendt mentions Giambattista Vico, whose despair made him abandon the natural sciences and turn to the field of history. Vico came to the realization that physical truth is reserved only for the Creator of the world, and in contrast, historical truth can be known to man; therefore, it can be "made." Arendt, *Between Past and Future*, 57. In his book *La scienza nuova* (1725), Vico refers to history as a manufactured object. He is therefore an example of the development of this modern historical consciousness that united nature and history and, in fact, he became one of the fathers of modern historical consciousness. In the field of modern political philosophy, Arendt indicates Thomas Hobbes as a representative of what used to be a new trend that used "the process," which invaded the natural sciences through the experiment in which natural processes are artificially imitated in the same way as a principle of action in the realm of human affairs. In Hobbes's theory, this happens in introspection, through which one discovers internal processes of emotions and turns them into automatic rules of life in the state ("Leviathan"). Hobbes's political philosophy was actually an attempt to build devices by which a state could be made into an artificial animal.

to nature, in the modern age, nature and human history were united through their transformation into "processes."

3. Reversal between means and ends. In Aristotelian terms, the "process" of making something disappears in the final product, which is the traditional experience of *homo faber*, who emphasized the priority of the final product over the production process; he saw the process as a means to an end. Whereas in the modern version of *homo faber*, the scientist only wants to know. The applicability of his discoveries does not interest him.[17]

It was found that in response to the despair of understanding things that were not created by man (nature)—despair of ever finding the truth—modern man concentrated all his practical abilities to the maximum, so that every time man acts, he starts a process.[18]

THE DESTRUCTION OF CONTEMPLATION

As mentioned, it is not that the rise of the "active life" as an action in a production form (*homo faber*'s mentality) simply took the place of "contemplative life." Rather, the introduction of the idea of "the process" into action made the contemplation meaningless in our lives, and *homo faber* won over the prodigal.

How did it happen? Arendt explains that in ancient Greek thought, contemplation was essential to *homo faber* because he creates something according to an idea that stands before his eyes before starting to work, and at the end as he evaluates the finished product. According to Plato, the craftsman did not come up with this model himself. It was given to human cognition, and

17. This inversion was hidden at the beginning of the modern age, which was dominated by a mechanistic worldview, a favorite of *homo faber*. At this stage, the idea of process was limited, meaning that nature as a whole was still seen as the finished product of a divine creator. The situation was like a clock: the movements of the dials are particular natural processes, but the nature of the clock itself as an object is arbitrary in the mind of the craftsman who created it. In nature, it is God.

18. Arendt, *Between Past and Future*, 62.

the craftsman only imitates it. Hence, this model is permanent and supreme in a way that is not realized in material. The craft decays and spoils this model that was eternal as long as it was an object for contemplation only. That observation of a model which intended to guide the creation of an object without taking action is not "wonder" (Greek: *thaumazein*) or "theory" in the face of the miracle of Being which puts a person in stasis, but is, rather, a deliberate pause in the activity of doing through which one reaches a state of contemplation. The beautiful and eternal cannot be made of matter. While wonder without speech is the property of a minority of philosophers, the contemplative observation of the craftsman is known to many.

Since *homo faber* was familiar with the pleasure of contemplation, this was not a radical turn for him but merely to embrace and extend his gaze to the model (*eidos*) that he had previously sought to imitate. Now he knows that trying to embody matter will only corrupt him. Hence, Arendt again explains that it is not only that doing took the place of contemplation at the top of the hierarchy of the constellation, but the constellation itself was broken because of the emphasis on the process instead of the product and its eternal fixed model. There is a transition from the question "what" the thing is and what to produce to the question "how" and through what process the thing comes into being, with the aim of reproducing it. There is a loss of faith that contemplation yields truth, and therefore contemplation has no place already in "active life" and in normal human experience in general.[19]

CONNECTING HISTORY AND NATURE INTO A FABRICATED PRODUCT

Since the beginning of the twentieth century, technology has appeared as a common basis for the natural sciences and history. And this is completely in line with the intention of modern science.[20]

19. Arendt, *Human Condition*, 274–78.

20. Arendt, *Between Past and Future*, 58–59.

Action (in the form of production) and technology have linked nature to history in an unprecedented way that created a common form of technology that we use to produce an impact on our world. Unlike the things in nature and the human individual lives that shaped the flow of history, the "modern concept of history" marks the transformation of history into a manufactured object that owes its existence exclusively to the human race, and is able to provide certain knowledge (as Heisenberg said). This history no longer consists of the actions and sufferings of people; people's life story has turned into an artificial process. In other words, Western humanity has come to believe that it can only rely on the work of its own hands, and that a sustainable shared life is only possible in a manufactured world populated by isolated individuals who each believe they control their own destiny. The modern historian is not looking for facts, reality, or truth. Nowadays historians make history just as scientists make nature. The modern historian is a scientist who starts a process and gives it a name that will be useful. And if this is so, Arendt continues, then it is understandable why history—as both an academic discipline and a field of interest to ordinary people—is in decline in the modern age. After all, why study history if it doesn't exist? It is more important to produce it than to learn it.

THE LOSS OF SCIENTIFIC OBJECTIVITY

Along with introspection in philosophy and the parallel trend of internalization in science, "the process" is another version of subjectivism; that is, the "modern concept of history" marks a loss of objectivity in the natural sciences and the science of history, an objectivity that characterized the Greek historians.[21] As long as

21. Unlike the impartiality of the ancient Greeks, who regarded the achievement itself regardless of who achieved it (even the enemy), the scientific attempts of the moderns are framed by their own questions so that nature becomes a mirror view of themselves. This is modern subjectivism. With Cartesian doubt, a variety of points of view are meaningless. There is no real greatness in people or deeds. Instead, a new standard appears: there is no real greatness but only taste and preference, as Kant pointed out. And there are not

we seek to know the natural world through the experiments that humans create and operate, the quality of the knowledge we obtain is determined by human framing. This does not mean that the experiments we conduct are not professional. But they are always framed by our questions, so that nature always becomes a mirror image of our hypotheses.

THE "PROCESS" IDEA IS ANTI-POLITICAL

As in the Aristotelian model, where the process of making an object disappears in the final product, the processes that moderns begin are invisible and are only deduced through abstract analysis from visible phenomena. The "story" is more important than the reality. In short: the "process" replaced Being.

The idea that only what I am about to do will be realistic and actual is legitimate in the field of creative work, but it is not suitable for an actual course of events where everything is unpredictable. Acting through doing and thinking through "reckoning with results" is ignoring the unpredictable factor of events occurring in political life.[22] The result of the distortion of "action" is that we have reached a situation today where everyone who "acts" actually starts a process without even being aware of it. It is not by chance that the word "entrepreneurship" has become commonplace. Indeed, Arendt concludes, Hegel's gigantic enterprise to reconcile

---

necessarily historical events; namely, there is nothing that really deserves to be remembered. History is simply one process we tell, and we can tell many others. And what we tell is not driven by the greatness of historical events but by their usefulness, and thus history loses its objectivity and becomes a technology—that is, something through which we wanted to achieve our ends.

22. Even before the modern discovery of history, Thomas Hobbes introduced the idea that the state is an engine that moves itself like a clock, and the feelings revealed in introspection are the automatic life measure of the state ("Leviathan"). However, this mechanistic approach that introduces new concepts of action and calculation into human affairs does not suit the unpredictable nature of political life, as it is impossible to calculate with certainty an occurrence that cannot be known in advance. According to Arendt, Hobbes's theory is an example of how modern political philosophy struggles to reconcile reason and reality, which were separated.

spirit with reality was based on the fact that reason was separated from reality.[23] And this also explains the crisis of "the life of contemplation," which ended in its elimination. According to Arendt, what finally ended contemplation was not *homo faber's* rise to the top of the hierarchy of human activity but rather the introduction of the concept of process into action. In the activity of creation, the emphasis shifted from the final product and the fixed guide model to the process of the creation; from the question of "what" the thing itself is and what kind of thing must be produced, to the question of "how" and in what processes the thing comes into being and how it can be reproduced.

23. Arendt, *Human Condition*, 274.

CHAPTER 6

The Transition to the "Modern World" and Mass Society

THE LAST TWO REVERSALS in Arendt's narrative of modernity are the fall of the *homo faber* model and the rise of the last social model of humanity, which heralded the transition from the "modern age" to the "modern world" we live in today: the *animal laborans*.[1] Although the salient features of the modern age from its beginning were the typical attitudes of the *homo faber*,[2] meaning that the conditions were very favorable for him, he did not survive. And unlike the drama of his victory, his defeat was gradual, a chain of deviations from his traditional mentality.[3]

HOMO FABER IN A WORLD OF PROCESSES

The belief that "man can only know what he has done himself" that led to the victory of *homo faber* is the same belief behind the principle of "the process," which finally destroyed him. The categories of "the process" are foreign to the needs and ideals of the *homo faber*. The modern transition from the "what" to the "how," from

1. I am following sections 43–45 in the last chapter of *The Human Condition*.

2. Arendt, *Human Condition*, 279.

3. Arendt, *Human Condition*, 285.

the thing itself to its production process, deprived *homo faber* of stable measures and measurements that always provided him with guidelines for judgment. In the previous chapter, we saw that man began to regard himself as an inseparable part of two all-embracing superhuman processes: nature and history. Both were doomed to an endless progression without a purpose, an end ("telos").[4] Both of these processes are in constant motion, and whenever they achieve some kind of stability, some kind of telos, they must continue even though it does not lead to any higher meaning. Therefore, there is no value to the production operation of the *homo faber*. In this world of processes, he has no place because he does not produce permanent things anymore. This is, of course, a kind of alienation from the world: if the purpose of the *work* is to create things that will last and make our world common (objects, institutions, etc.), then with the loss of permanent objects, we lose the world. And, as mentioned, we turn the world into ourselves.[5]

Arendt indicates additional reasons for the deviation from *homo faber*'s mentality, which led to his defeat.

THE COMMERCIAL SOCIETY

The development of commercial society, or consumer society, and the victory of exchange value over utility value that instilled the principle that everything is exchangeable, also "contributed" to the emptying of *homo faber*'s work of meaning. This relativity led to nihilism—a devaluation of all values. There is no absolute value; everything is relative to its exchange rate for something else. Again, the role of the *work* to create things that will last and make

4. Arendt, *Human Condition*, 280.

5. The principle of utility still presupposes a world in which objects are of use to man. As soon as objects are not valued first of all for their usefulness but as random results of the production process that brought them into existence, so that the final product is no longer a real purpose but a means to produce something else, then these objects are secondary. This is the nihilism (devaluation of all values) in *homo faber*'s concept, which mainly produces tools to produce other tools and only incidentally produces objects. Arendt, *Human Condition*, 281–82.

our world common is nullified in a world where everything is a potential candidate for consumption. The modern man no longer builds a house and buys furniture that he intends to bequeath to his descendants. He rather buys it in order to sell it and make a profit. With such a mindset, it is impossible to talk about a stable, permanent political world—a common home.[6]

THE ELIMINATION OF CONTEMPLATION

As mentioned, contemplation is essential to *homo faber* because he creates an object according to an idea that stands before his eyes. The meaning of the transition from the question "what" the thing is and what to produce to the question "how" and in what process the thing comes into being—in order to reproduce it—led to the abandonment of contemplation as something that yields truth and, in fact, to the elimination of contemplation from "active life." Without the contemplation factor, the *homo faber* functions as an *animal laborans*.

FROM UTILITARIANISM TO "HAPPINESS"

The essence of *homo faber*'s worldview is utilitarianism, which is based on the principle of use value. This meaning was changed to the principle of "the greatest happiness for the greatest number of people" that was formulated by the English philosopher Jeremy Bentham.[7] According to this principle, the question of usefulness is found outside the production process. The determining standard is no longer utility and usefulness but "happiness" in the sense of calculating the amount of pain and pleasure experienced in the

6. Arendt writes, "The industrial revolution has replaced all *work* with *labor*, and the result has been that the things of the modern world have become labor products whose natural fate is to be consumed, instead of work products which are there to be used . . . a chair or a table is now consumed as rapidly as a dress and a dress used up almost as quickly as food." Arendt, *Human Condition*, 108.

7. Bentham, *Principles of Morals*, 27.

production or consumption of things.[8] As a result, the meaning of the use is now not to encourage productivity but to reduce the pain and effort in the labor process.

Arendt thus accuses Bentham of radically emptying the idea of utilitarianism, the guiding line of *homo faber*, into vulgar and hedonistic modern hedonism.[9] In its original sense, utility still presupposes that there is a world of objects, i.e., it refers to a common world, whereas Bentham changed it into consideration of pleasure and suffering (happiness) that bring us completely into our minds (introspection). In fact, in Arendt's opinion, usefulness has become universal egoism.[10]

As we shall see later, without a higher source of meaning, technology and industrial modernity gave rise to mass societies dominated by the individual and collective instrumental pursuit of interests, where in his spare time the toiling individual (the laborer) never spent anything but on consumption. Which led to the

8. In his "calculus of pain and pleasure," Bentham introduced a mathematical method into the field of morality. According to this calculation, happiness is the sum of the pleasures minus the pains, which is actually introspection—namely, an inner sense that perceives sensations detached from worldly objects. According to Bentham, humans do not share the world in common, but human nature, which is expressed in the fact that the calculation and the effect of pain and pleasure are the same for everyone. Bentham, *Principles of Morals*, 14–15.

9. Arendt comments that the modern Bentham-following hedonist does not come close to the spirit and self-discipline, fanatical righteousness, and nobility of character of the ancient Stoics and Epicureans. The modern world has already succumbed to hedonistic egoism. Arendt, *Human Condition*, 282.

10. The meaning of "happiness" in Arendt's discussion here has nothing to do with *eudaimonia*, i.e., a consciousness that is achieved when life is "well lived," but a private perception of physical comfort whose measure is utilitarian. Life in late modern society is characterized by an unprecedented emphasis on physical well-being and an equally unprecedented fear of pain or suffering and discomfort. Most contemporary science, be it through medicine or other means, is aimed at eliminating suffering and discomfort. The "happy person" behaves politely, like a reconciled person who has lost the ability to act. As an activity dictated by rules, his behavior is therefore never innovative. Not the *homo faber* or the man of action, but only the *animal laborans* demand to be happy or think that mortal man can and should be happy.

fact that no object in the world will be safe from consumption and thus to destruction.

THE "PRINCIPLE OF LIFE"

Homo faber's idea that we make things was defeated by the "happiness principle." But according to Arendt, what really stands behind Bentham's "Utilitarianism," as well as the other versions of modern hedonism, is not happiness but a much stronger principle: life itself. The purpose is the promotion of individual life and the survival of the human race. According to Arendt, this philosophy that raises life itself as the measure of everything is vulgar and uncritical.

CHRISTIANITY AND THE SECULAR MODERN IDEAL OF "LIFE AS THE HIGHEST GOOD"

So far, we have discussed the chain of events (science, finding an Archimedean point in the universe, introspection through philosophy, reversals in the constellation of the human condition) that led to the reduction of humanity's ambition to a single, animal interest: staying alive. Arendt now provides another reason for this, perhaps the most important, and turns again to Christianity and, as last time, here too it is not a theological discussion, as one would expect.[11] According to Arendt, life has become a point of reference and the ideal of the "good" of modern age because the whole thing called "modernity" took place within a Christian culture.

Christianity revolutionized the ancient world when it elevated individual life to an immortal status equal to that of nature. A status that, according to the Greeks, belonged to the universe alone. And this is actually, according to Arendt, the meaning of the "good news" of Christianity that brought about its victory—namely, to give hope in a world doomed to destruction. Mortal man, the most worthless and hopeless creature in the universe, received an immortal soul through the Messiah. It certainly brings him some

11. I am following section 44 in the last chapter of *The Human Condition*.

hope. And so, according to Christian theology, although life in this world is a miserable initial stage, it is nevertheless a condition for eternal life. Arendt's point is that Christianity subordinated political action to necessity, a necessary evil intended only to correct human sins and preserve "earthly interests." Instead of the political body, which according to the Greeks should last, the life of the individual moved to the center. Aspiration for immortality in this world, fame, and so on, has become an empty illusion. From now on, everything is about necessity. And in this new world, there is no more contempt for laborers, slaves, or those who simply want to stay alive. In fact, we appreciate them. In terms of the category of "active life," the immortality that Christianity gave to the life of the individual soul also led to a lack of interest in the world (alienation from the world), something that was reinforced in the Middle Ages when the "life of contemplation" was elevated to the top of the hierarchy of human activities as a life with justification.

However, the fact that the ideal of the sanctity of life is Christian in origin and has influenced modern Western culture does not mean that we still live in a Christian world. It is clear that Christianity as a faith was hit hardest by the Cartesian doubt—for example, in Pascal and Kierkegaard. Unlike the onslaught of vulgar materialism in the nineteenth century, Cartesian doubt made the Christian promise downright absurd.

"HUMAN RIGHTS" AS A SUPREME VALUE

According to Arendt, this upgrading of "life" is destructive to politics.

Politics, that strives for earthly immortality, was made a device to keep people alive in the name of the value of "human rights." The problem with turning "human rights" into a value is as follows: the political community is the arena for the application of freedom. Freedom is not just another aspect of politics, like justice, equality, power, etc. Rather, it is the main reason for people to organize themselves into a political body. Freedom is the *raison d'être* of politics, and without it, it has no meaning. Human rights have become the essence of modern politics because we no longer fully believe in any other political projects such as communism, socialism, liberalism, etc. The only thing we fully believe in today is keeping people alive. Yet "human rights" are the lowest political form[12] because if all we agree on about politics is keeping people alive, we won't achieve anything politically; we won't create great things; in fact, we won't build anything.[13]

And here we actually reach the final conclusion that connects all the parts of the book *The Human Condition*—namely, that with the defeat of *homo faber*, the last reversal of Arendt's story takes place: the rise of the *animal laborans*, which, like the splitting of the atom in the field of science, constitutes the transition from the "modern age" to the "modern world" in which we've lived up to now.

12. This topic is connected to her book on totalitarianism, in which she discusses the issue of refugees in Europe during World War II. Arendt, *Origins of Totalitarianism*, vol. 2, ch. 9. Arendt's argument is that "human rights" is an abstract concept that is difficult to define precisely from a legal point of view. Even if one tried—and there are even democratic policies that are based on this idea—this did not help the masses of refugees who lost their place in the world, and the nation-states had difficulty responding to this. Therefore, Arendt claims that if a person has these "rights," then this is only one political right, namely that his words be heard and matter for others.

13. Arendt's alleged disdain for human rights and, at the same time, her appreciation of human greatness and pluralism may seem Nietzschean. Nevertheless, she is not saying that we should sacrifice certain numbers of people for the sake of better politics. Her point is rather that in a pluralistic society, the celebration of a single value should not come at the price of overlooking all other things we value. For example, in Germany, Angela Merkel's immigration policy prioritized the preservation of refugees over the republic's security. This led to right-wing extremism on the brink of fascism. During the COVID-19 crisis, many opposed the restriction policies of the experts in the health community and wanted to make decisions for themselves about whether to meet their relatives. During the first lockdowns in Italy, Giorgio Agamben indicated that it illustrates what he calls "bare life," namely a rejection of Christian and Western values such as family, friendships, worship, community, etc., and raising the value of keeping people alive at any cost. Agamben's critique is consistent with Arendt's thesis on the victory of the *animal laborans* and the victory of the principle of life as the supreme good. And it corresponds to her argument in regard to "the Royal Society" as a model of the powerful alienated standpoint of science in the realm of ordinary human affairs.

CHAPTER 7

Mass Society as a Political
Problem of the "Modern World"

ACCORDING TO ARENDT, THE *animal laborans* won because of secularization and the loss of faith in immortality due to Cartesian doubt.[1] Human life has returned to being finite as in ancient pagan culture, although in a modern world that is less stable and permanent, without objects that are meant to endure, a world that is hard to trust as in the Christian era.[2] Following are two examples of what Christianity left behind.

First, the only potentially immortal thing that remains in modern life is life itself, in the sense of the life process of the human race that can go on forever.[3] This is very different from the

1. I am following section 45 in the last part of *The Human Condition*.

2. The Greeks thought that immortal life arose from the world, and the Christians believe that it came from the eternal soul. But because of Cartesian doubt, moderns no longer believe in the immortality of individual life (the soul) nor in the immortality of the world. The world is becoming less reliable. That is why man is thrown back on himself instead of on the world. It is commonly thought that secularism means that we don't care about God and focus on this world. And Arendt says that we don't care about the world, either, but about ourselves. What remains are the desires of our body that we confuse with passion. We see them as irrational because we cannot calculate them, and so we are gradually leaving behind the common world of reason and turning to the world of physical desires.

3. Instead of the classical economy in which individuals act out of

immortality of the life of the individual Christian in the Middle Ages, and the political body in antiquity.

Secondly, because Christians treated *labor*, *work*, and *action* equally, they essentially redeemed *labor* from its despised image in antiquity by seeing it as something necessary for the preservation of biological life.[4]

Since individual life has become a part of the life process, all that is required is to toil and survive as an individual and a family, which is the distinct characteristic of *animal laborans*.[5] *Action* and *work*, the higher activities, are not necessary to bind the individual to the life of the human race. Therefore, the *action* was swallowed up within the natural force of the "life process" itself, and the role of the *homo faber* was mistakenly taken by the *animal laborans*.[6] In short, everything that is not necessary for life and that is not related to survival and metabolism in nature has become unnecessary. For example, art exists only for those who can afford it; it has been relegated to an exceptional category. The point is that culture has

---

self-interest, the situation after the rise of the "social" is one of single-interest rule: the classes, or the human race, but not individual human beings. Marx talked about the forces of interests that motivate and direct the classes in society, and the conflict between them directs the whole society together.

4. In ancient times, there was contempt for the slave who served the needs of life and was subordinate to his master because he wanted to "stay alive." However, there is no evidence in Christian writings for glorifying labor either. The reason that Christianity did not elevate labor to the level of an ideal is that, especially in Scholasticism in the Middle Ages, the "life of contemplation" was held as more influential.

5. The ancient Greeks had slaves so that aristocrats could occupy themselves with higher activities, such as politics, in their free time, and they needed violence for the purpose of exercising authority. The art of human violence toward humans was acceptable in tyrannical regimes and in wars where captives were turned into slaves, so that the slaves were already accustomed to violence. The modern age has reduced violence significantly, thus opening the door for a renewed entry of necessity, which appeared with the rise of the laborers' society. Arendt, *Human Condition*, 111–12.

6. We already discussed the confusion between action and work in the previous chapter. The action is mistakenly seen as a craft of creation and doing. The doing is seen as a more complex type of labor, but no more mysterious than it. In general, a common focus in the social sciences is dealing with items that change but retain their name.

been reduced to an entertainment industry.[7] Art is today viewed as a habit and a secondary good;[8] masterpieces are valued more for their status symbol than for their intrinsic value. In Arendt's view, this represents a shift in the human condition. Naturally, it has to do with the fact that we no longer view contemplation as a worthwhile endeavor. Because our major priority is the preservation of our species, we are unconcerned about geniuses or spirituality, thus none of the higher human qualities are more important. People practice yoga and meditation; while this may be beneficial, it is just one aspect of "life process."[9]

As mentioned, not only contemplation has become meaningless, but thought itself has become a "reckoning with consequences," meaning a brain function that electronic devices would perform better anyway.

As we have seen in the first reversal of the "active life," the one who replaced the "contemplative life" was not action in the sense of the ancient polis, but *homo faber*, who reduced the *action* to "doing" and "production," which is still about doing lasting

7. In the world of the *animal laborans*, people keep books at home as a status symbol. I indicated in the theoretical background section that the objects created by *homo faber*, such as architecture, fine art, politics, etc., were meant to remain in the world for generations and be assimilated into the collective memory. This is what builds our artificial political world. And of all the objects, the work of art is the highest because it was intended in advance for preservation only. According to Arendt, for those who are content with reading summaries of masterpieces, and even translations, it is better not to read at all because reading not in the original does not preserve an object.

8. Arendt writes, "We live in a society of laborers. This society did not come about through the emancipation of the laboring classes but by the emancipation of laboring activity itself. . . . Whatever we do, we are supposed to do for the sake of 'making a living.' The same trend to level down all serious activities to the status of making a living is manifest in contemporary labor theories which define labor as the opposite of play. . . . In these theories, not even the work of the artist is left. It is dissolved into play and has lost its worldly meaning. The playfulness of the artist is felt to fulfil the same function in the laboring life process of society as the playing of tennis or the pursuit of a hobby fulfils in the life of the individual." Arendt, *Human Condition*, 110–11.

9. The social man has one law: comfort, or life. What remains to be controlled is the life process. We only care about the laws of economics and sociology—how we govern ourselves to maximize the usefulness of the species.

things in the world, which makes it common. But in the "modern world" of *animal laborans*, we only produce useful things for the preservation of the household, the body, etc.—namely, transitory things for survival, which are not related to something that will last. However, not only the actions of the *homo faber* were reduced to those of the *animal laborans*, but even *labor* has become a job,[10] meaning that we have reached a situation where getting rid of *labor* is not utopia.

THE EVENT OF AUTOMATION AND ITS CONSEQUENCES

In a reality where individual lives have been swallowed up in an all-encompassing life process, the only decision left is when to stop a bit, rest, and improve comfort in the toil process to reduce the pain we still feel as individuals; in short, immerse oneself in automatic functional behaviorism and work as if "drugged." Yet another decisive event changed this too: the advent of automation, which will soon probably empty the factories and free the human race from the most natural and ancient nuisance of toil and binding to necessity. Liberation from *labor* itself is not new. It used to be the privilege of a minority. In the ancient Greek polis, slaves freed the landlord to engage in the sublime activity of political action in the public sphere.

The modern age theoretically glorified toil, which turned the whole society into a "society of toilers." Today, it seems that technological advances and developments are used to literally eliminate the toil, an achievement that previous generations could only

10. This corresponds with the section on the undercover agent, known as Lawrence of Arabia, from Arendt's *The Origins of Totalitarianism*, 2:343. Lawrence retreated into his individuality behind an effort to bind himself to forces beyond human control—namely, a kind of English victory in the war. He was swept into the current of historical necessity and thereby became a missionary or an agent of the world-dominating cosmic forces. The only pleasure he could derive from this was that some mighty movement had adopted him and swept him along. Lawrence has become part of a stream of history, which is an expression of the Archimedean point being applied to ourselves.

dream about. However, according to Arendt, fulfilling this wish is a self-defeating act, because we deal with a society that does not recognize other significant activities for which it is appropriate to win freedom from *labor*. Even presidents, kings, and prime ministers today think of their job in terms of a job that is necessary for social life. That is to say that politicians have become laborers too. They care about their personal careers and the general survival of their people, and they provide them with comfort with the help of technology instead of dealing with building correct politics.[11]

Among intellectuals, only a few still see their occupation as a real, meaningful work and not just a livelihood. The modern *animal laborans* does not deserve free time because he is unable to use it for a noble purpose. When contemplation isn't interesting, what's left is to lie on couches and watch movies on TV. With the absence of contemplation, everything means lust. Eat delicious fast food and watch TV like Roman aristocrats who spent their days lying on beds eating grapes.[12] It is not the *homo faber* or the man

11. Arendt writes, "The *animal laborans* was permitted to occupy the public realm; and yet, as long as the *animal laborans* remains in possession of it, there can be no true public realm, but only private activities displayed in the open." Arendt, *Human Condition*, 114–15. Arendt explains that the fact that the liberation of labor did not lead to freedom but fulfilled the fear that all humanity would fall under the yoke of necessity, "was already clearly perceived by Marx when he insisted that the aim of a revolution could not possibly be the already-accomplished emancipation of the laboring classes, but must consist in the emancipation of man from labor. At first glance, this aim seems Utopian, and the only strictly Utopian element in Marx's teachings. Emancipation from labor, in Marx's own terms, is emancipation from necessity . . . which is the very condition of human life." Arendt, *Human Condition*, 113.

12. Arendt writes, "This ideal of modern society but the age-old dream of the poor and destitute . . . turns into a fool's paradise as soon as it is realized. The hope that inspired Marx and the best men of the various workers' movements—that free time eventually will emancipate men from necessity . . . rests on the illusion of a mechanistic philosophy which assumes that labor power, like any other energy, can never be lost, so that if it is not spent and exhausted in the drudgery of life it will automatically nourish other, 'higher,' activities. The guiding model of this hope in Marx was doubtless the Athens of Pericles which, in the future, with the help of the vastly increased productivity of human labor, would need no slaves. . . . A hundred years after Marx we know the fallacy of this reasoning; the spare time of the *animal laborans* is never spent

of *action*, but the *animal laborans* who demands to be happy or think that "man should be happy." Arendt reminds us that "the human condition is such that pain and effort are not just symptoms which can be removed without changing life itself; they are rather the modes in which life itself, together with necessity to which it is bound, makes itself felt. For mortals, the 'easy life of the gods' would be a lifeless life."[13] Within this society, which is egalitarian because equality is the way in which labor makes people live together, there are no longer classes, no aristocracy with a political or spiritual character, from which the other human capacities can be reconstructed. In the face of this distortion, it should be taken into account that the elimination of the "elite" also comes at a price of a life without truth and depth. We are currently faced with the appearance of a society of laborers without *labor*, the only activity left to them. Obviously, concludes Arendt, it can't get any worse than that.[14]

The point in the discussion here on Arendt's critique of mass society can be articulated from another point of view. Arendt was an advocate of participatory democracy, her inspiration being the model of the Greek polis. This politics that she admires was made possible by the use of slaves who freed the landlords to engage in it. As we know, modernity brought with it a tendency to break down many cultural and social barriers to equality—that is,

---

in anything but consumption, and the more time left to him, the greedier and more craving his appetites. That these appetites become more sophisticated, so that consumption is no longer restricted to the necessities but, on the contrary, mainly concentrates on the superfluities of life, does not change the character of this society, but harbors the grave danger that eventually no object of the world will be safe from consumption and annihilation through consumption." Arendt, *Human Condition*, 114–15.

13. Arendt, *Human Condition*, 103–4.

14. Arendt, *Human Condition*, 5. Arendt indicates, "The easier that life has become in a consumers' or laborers' society, the more difficult it will be to remain aware of the urges of necessity by which it is driven, even when pain and effort, the outward manifestations of necessity, are hardly noticeable at all. The danger is that such a society, dazzled by the abundance of its growing fertility and caught in the smooth functioning of a never-ending process, would no longer be able to recognize its own futility." Arendt, *Human Condition*, 116–17.

strived to eliminate sources of inequality. Francis Fukuyama suggests that modern natural science was, in fact, invented by slaves who were forced to work and disliked their current situation, not by idle masters who had everything they wanted. Through science and technology, the slave discovers that he can change not only the physical environments into which he is born, but also his own nature.[15] Against this historical argument, Arendt would say that freedom through technology alone is politically inauthentic. That is to say that the social political advancement (liberal democracy) that technological advancement brought about, can remain hollow. Moreover, technological advancement can also exist without political advancement, as seen today in authoritarian regimes like Russia.

15. Fukuyama, *End of History*, 194.

Chapter 8

Transferring the Weight of Action from Politics to Science

THE GOOD NEWS, ACCORDING to Arendt, is that humanity has not completely lost the ability to act. After all, people continue to create and build like *homo faber*, albeit in a significantly decreased manner.

The ability to act authentically in the sense of releasing processes has become the property of a minority of scientists, smaller than the community of artists who also know how to act in the sense of starting something new; for example, the scientists erased the traditional protective border between nature and the human world through the "processes." Although they have been working on it for a long time already, away from the spotlight in quiet laboratories, their achievements turn out to be more politically significant than those who are called "statesmen" or "politicians." It is only ironic that precisely those whom public opinion has always regarded as impractical and non-political turned out to be the only people today who still know how to act, even in coordination with each other. Since the founding of "the Royal Society" in the seventeenth century with the aim of conquering nature, scientists have accumulated today, in the "modern world," great political power.

On the other hand, although scientists have the most power to "act" freely today, unfortunately they work into nature from a perspective from the universe that ignores the networks of relationships in the field of human affairs, and therefore their action lacks the revelatory nature of the *action*. Their action into nature lacks the ability to tell stories with meaning for humans—something that illuminates human life, and thus becoming a historical *action*.[1] After all, science is only a craft, the art of *homo faber*. As such, it has the power to fundamentally alter nature's laws and bring about true revolutions. However, its output is limited to tools, which indeed last, but have no inherent meaning independent of humans. The moon and Sputnik are both bodies caught in an earth-centered gravitational orbit; the laws of modern physics do not distinguish between them. It is the human element that separates them—for example, the meaning of Sputnik in the race to colonize space and get away from earth.

We saw before that, according to Arendt, the earth is a central condition of the "human condition" and earthly nature. Human artifice separates man from all other living things. But life itself exists outside the artificial world that man has built on earth. And through life, man maintains a relationship with all living organisms in nature. It is evident that today scientists are making efforts to make this life artificial as well. They are on their way to establishing a society that rebels against the limitations of nature, as it was given to us as a gift from nowhere, which marks the cutting of man's last connection to the company of natural things. According to Arendt, the same desire to escape the prison of the earth is motivating attempts to replicate the miracle of life in test tubes in hopes of making a superman by modifying his form and function. Although such ambitions are still in the future, the boomerang effect of the victories of modern science is felt, as we have already seen, in the crisis of the natural sciences. Although the "truths" of this scientific worldview can be presented in mathematical formulas and proven through technology, it is not possible to express them

---

1. The internalization and alienation of people from the world keeps the scientists very involved in the world because they can inject their mental power. But for many people who are not scientists, the world they see every day is not real, and they remain adrift, without meaning or purpose.

in normal language and thought. We, as earth-bound creatures who began to act as if we were inhabitants of the universe, are no longer able to think and talk about things that we are able to do. Since knowledge, in the modern sense of "knowing how," is detached from cognition, we will indeed require artificial machines to conduct the thinking and speaking for us in order to monitor what we do.[2] Thought has become meaningless unless it is used for calculation. Yet Arendt distinguishes between the brain and the mind.[3] The latter is replaced by the brain. Thus, judgmental thought becomes the highest activity in correct politics and hence relevant to the future of the world.

The technical ability to implement this vision of the scientists is already here. But according to Arendt the question here is a first-rate political one—namely, whether we want to leave the decision on the direction of the use of our scientific and technological knowledge to professional scientists and politicians. To put it bluntly, Arendt wants to say that if we ask a physicist if he is aware of the possible devastating consequences of his research for the earth, we will find that he is aware, but he will do it anyway because he cares more about whether what he has been working on all his life will work or not.

Along with the forces of capitalism through the consumption of technology, science now enjoys unprecedented power. But the order that makes this possible is irrelevant to politics. Arendt therefore recommends not trusting the political judgment of scientists, not because they refused to oppose the development of atomic weapons, but precisely because they operate in a world where speech has lost its power—that is, a non-political world. After all,

2. Arendt, *Human Condition*, 2–4.

3. The phenomenon of "reckoning with results" is connected to Arendt's analysis of the problems in contemporary education. She argues that the focus of education nowadays is on reasoning—which is a typical feature of science— rather than judgmental thinking, which is crucial for political life. The younger generation is more content with their information and less opinionated. They reason everything, including negative things. Thus, all that is left are fragments of politics—groups existing separately in thinner worlds.

everything that a person experiences or knows will only be significant to the extent that it can be talked about or told in a story.

To summarize, the previous two chapters direct to one point:
alienation from the world, distancing the public from the objects
toward a story process and the "how" of the objects that are in our
mind. We don't want to interfere with the world. We simply want
to make money and consume things, travel around the world, and,
in short, run away from home rather than make it a place we want
to live in. We gave up action and democracy; we act less politically because we want to understand and better the world through
science, not as something given to us.[4] The impact of science on
politics and society today is expressed in the technocracy of the
"social" sphere, which stifles free political activity. Instead of working into politics, for example, creating a new political system, the
professional politicians, who have lost the knowledge of how to act
in the sense of starting something new, use scientists and "plumb-
ers," as Arendt calls them, meaning those who are looking for how

4. Construction planning in small countries like Israel demonstrates the
issues of processes and the adoption of an Archimedean point of view. Indeed,
it shows the takeover of the technological-scientific consideration over the
government in action. The alliance between private entrepreneurs, planning
committees, and government officials who sell a false vision of building towers
to solve population density is symptomatic of adopting an Archimedean point
of view that ignores the interests of citizens at the local level. Apart from the
fact that it is housing that only the rich can afford and is actually intended to
increase local government profits through increasing taxes, the standardization of new construction erases the traditional uniqueness of places and architecture that used to produce a sense of durability that is necessary for common
political body. Although Arendt's use of the term "nature" is not related to
ecology and environment, I think that in the case of damage to the natural
balance through excessive road construction and obsessive construction, Arendt is nevertheless relevant. This phenomenon echoes Heisenberg's words,
stating that "today man meets only things he made himself. There are still parts
of the earth that remain natural. But here too man will intervene sooner or
later." Heisenberg, *Conception of Nature*, 23–24. It also corresponds with the
environmentalist Bill McKibben's claim that we are on the verge of destroying
the natural realm that human activity has not yet touched and manipulated.
The construction of too many roads and obsessive construction can harm the
natural balance and contribute to environmental degradation. McKibben, *End
of Nature*.

to translate the discoveries of science into profit, to sell the public the image that "something good is happening; we are making progress." In Arendt's words, "the 'plumber', the technicians, who account today for the overwhelming majority of all 'researchers', have brought the results of the scientists down to earth."[5] While embracing the scientists' Archimedean point of view, politicians are led by the nose without comprehending, just as scientists are unaware of what they are capable of executing.

5. Arendt, *Between Past and Future*, 268.

Epilogue

IN THE INTRODUCTION I described Arendt's perception of modern science and technology as a combination of utopian and dystopian approaches. In her essay "The Conquest of Space and the Stature of Man," which appeared a few years after *The Human Condition*, she concludes that the conquest of space did not upgrade the rate of human stature. We dreamed of escaping from the earth, and we were thrown back with greater force into the imprisonment of the world we created in our minds.[1]

She continues,

> Man hoped he could travel to the Archimedean point, which he found with the help of abstraction and imagination. But in doing so . . . Man can only get lost in the universe because the only true Archimedean point is the void behind the universe.[2]

Furthermore, the degeneration of thinking into reckoning with consequences brought man back to an animal rank "from which, since Darwin, he imagines he has come."[3] Arendt's main argument is that the modern attempt to liberate man from his existence on earth was a mistake. The vision of space imperialism is synonymous with dehumanization. Indeed, modern man's incredible abilities could only be achieved by distancing himself from earth. However, the Archimedean wish comes at the cost

1. Arendt, *Between Past and Future*, 274.

2. Arendt, *Between Past and Future*, 272.

3. Arendt, *Human Condition*, 295.

of losing reality.[4] It alienated man from his immediate earthly surroundings,[5] and this disconnection from the common world marks the loss of truth and shared center.

Along with this disappointing report, she expressed in the same essay optimism that the time for political action has not finally passed, even in a world where the two qualitative activities that build politics have been swallowed up in seemingly natural "processes."[6] Arendt is not nostalgic; she does not think that it is possible or necessary to return to the Aristotelian concept of "wonder" and awe at nature that dominated the pre-modern era.[7] The "modern world" is a place that has already been profoundly shaped by technology, to the extent that when watched from a far Archimedean point in the universe, our activities, for example motorization, "would appear like a process of biological mutation in which human bodies gradually begin to be covered by shells of still."[8] In this irreversible reality, Arendt is concerned with the political question of how to imagine ways to redefine "active life" so that the constellation of relationships of our activities (the "human condition") will once again become worldly.

What Arendt is actually aiming at is a "new geocentrism" that will become possible if we accept ourselves as earthly beings and show care for our immediate environment, nature, and our political world. Indeed, the fact that we have become a society of

4. Arendt, *Human Condition*, 237–38.

5. Arendt, *Human Condition*, 228.

6. *Homo faber* was caught in an endless cycle of production and became an *animal laborans*. And the ability to act remains in the hands of some scientists whose activities are alienated from the political world. "The Modern World" is ruled by the *animal laborans*.

7. Contrary to thinkers such as Oswald Spengler and Heidegger, who saw Soviet Russia and the USA as guilty of leading the unbridled madness and hope of technological development and the organization of rootless human beings ("das Man" in Heidegger), i.e., a worldview as a struggle between authentic German culture and shallow Western and Soviet civilization, Arendt, despite Heidegger's renewed influence on her in his essay "The Question Concerning Technology" (1953), was not impressed by his fear of "Americanization," viewing technology as a characteristic of modernity in general.

8. Arendt, *Human Condition*, 295.

laborers who produce things that do not stay in the world long enough to be a part of it reflects this alienation from the world. Arendt clarifies that "our trust in the reality of life and in the reality of the world is not the same. The latter derives primarily from the permanence and durability of the world. . . . If one knew that the world would come to an end with or soon after his own death, it would lose all its reality, as it did for the early Christians as long as they were convinced of the immediate fulfillment of their eschatological expectations."[9]

Arendt's actual concern that the success of modern science and technology meant the loss of speech and, with it, all of politics—is now a reality in our society. In the Judeo-Christian tradition, as part of the relationship with God, it is permissible to pass criticism on the "manager" even if an answer is not always received. Today, giant technological businesses resemble semi-divine entities. The average consumer of their products and gadgets is continuously signing agreements with these corporations. Regardless of the service and transparency they offer, how many of us have the time and capacity to read a fifty-page handbook or contract? Can Arendt's humanitarian drive to become more geocentric again prevent the entrance of cosmic forces and substances into nature, and even into human affairs? Some post-humanists believe that the gap between man and technology can be bridged if we adapt human abilities to machines—for example, inserting chips with a computer-like level of computation into the human brain, creating a hybrid environment, and adapting the human ability to calculate to the level of "mathematization of science." However, Arendt, like Heidegger in his article "A Question Regarding Technology," was of the opinion that the solution to the question of technology cannot come from technology itself, such as spending a whole day playing with a smartphone to solve a problem about how to use it. If so, we should be concerned that, apart from Arendt and a small number of other serious philosophers, the intellectual effort to deal with the consequences of scientific and technological achievements has been insufficient because this topic is regarded

9. Arendt, *Human Condition*, 104.

as a problem for engineers and technologists. And worse than that: of politicians and scientists.

Bibliography

Agamben, Giorgio. *Homo Sacer: Sovereign Power and Bare Life*. Translated by Daniel Heller-Roazen. Stanford: Stanford University Press, 1998.

Arendt, Hannah. *Between Past and Future*. New York: Penguin, 2006.

———. *Crises of the Republic*. Harmondsworth, UK: Penguin, 1973.

———. *The Human Condition*. New York: Doubleday Anchor, 1959.

———. *The Life of the Mind*. New York: Harcourt, 1977.

———. *On Revolution*. London: Faber & Faber, 2016.

———. *The Origins of Totalitarianism*. New York: Meridian, 1958.

Bentham, Jeremy. *An Introduction to the Principles of Morals and Legislation*. Kitchener, Canada: Batoche, 2000. Originally published 1789.

Bezos, Jeff. "Human Population Will Grow to One Trillion." Interview by Lex Fridman. Lex Clips, YouTube, Dec. 18, 2023. https://www.youtube.com/watch?v=hZaOApuXLBE&t=54s.

Burtt, E. A. *The Metaphysical Foundations of Modern Science*. New York: Anchor, 1932.

Fukuyama, Francis. *The End of History and the Last Man*. New York: Avon, 1992.

Heidegger, Martin. "The Question Concerning Technology." In *The Question Concerning Technology and Other Essays*, 14–18. Translated by William Lovitt et al. New York: Garland, 1977.

Heisenberg, Werner. *The Physicist's Conception of Nature*. London: Hutchinson, 1958.

———. *Wandlungen in den Grundlagen der Naturwissenschaft*. Stuttgart: S. Hirzel, 1949.

Kant, Immanuel. "Universal Natural History and Theory of the Heavens, or Essay on the Constitution and the Mechanical Origin of the Whole Universe According to Newtonian Principles." In *Natural Science*, 182–308. Edited by Eric Watkins. Cambridge: Cambridge University Press, 2012.

Kierkegaard, Søren. *Philosophical Fragments, Johannes Climacus*. Edited and translated by H. V. Hong and E. H. Hong. Princeton: Princeton University Press, 1985.

Koyré, Alexandre. *From the Closed World to the Infinite Universe*. London: Johns Hopkins, 1957.

McKibben, Bill. *The End of Nature*. New York: Random, 1989.

Schrödinger, Erwin. *Nature and the Greeks and Science and Humanism*. London: Cambridge University Press, 1952.

Vico, Giambattista. *La scienza nuova*. Rome: Edizioni di Storia e Letteratura, 2023. Originally published 1725.

Weil, Simone. "Réflexions à propos de la théorie des quanta." *Cahiers du Sud* 51 (1942) 102–19.